# BestMasters

Springer awards „BestMasters“ to the best master's theses which have been completed at renowned Universities in Germany, Austria, and Switzerland.
The studies received highest marks and were recommended for publication by supervisors. They address current issues from various fields of research in natural sciences, psychology, technology, and economics.
The series addresses practitioners as well as scientists and, in particular, offers guidance for early stage researchers.

More information about this series at http://www.springer.com/series/13198

Verena Anna Berger

# Impact of Government Bonds Spreads on Credit Derivatives

## Analysis of Increasing Spreads Developments within the European Area

Springer Gabler

Verena Anna Berger
Vienna, Austria

OnlinePlus material to this book is available on
http://www.springer.com/978-3-658-20219-4

BestMasters
ISBN 978-3-658-20218-7 ISBN 978-3-658-20219-4 (eBook)
https://doi.org/10.1007/978-3-658-20219-4

Library of Congress Control Number: 2017960282

Springer Gabler


Printed on acid-free paper

This Springer Gabler imprint is published by Springer Nature
The registered company is Springer Fachmedien Wiesbaden GmbH
The registered company address is: Abraham-Lincoln-Str. 46, 65189 Wiesbaden, Germany

## Acknowledgements

I would like to thank my thesis supervisor, Mr. Hans Aubauer, who guided me along the path to completion of this thesis. Moreover, I thank my student colleagues as well as my friends, in particular Christina.

Most of all, I would like to thank my family. In particular, I am grateful for my parents, who supported me during my whole study time and who enabled me to go my way. My sincere thanks to my partner Alexander for his patient especially during the preparation of this work. Furthermore, I would like to thank my grandparents for their moral support during my study time.

# Institute's profile

## Master programme „Quantitative Asset and Risk Managment (ARIMA)“ at the University of Applied Science BFI Vienna

The University of Applied Sciences BFI Vienna offers the master's programme, "Quantitative Asset and Risk Management (ARIMA)", with the aim of providing students with an all-round understanding of the interaction between asset and risk management. Each of these functions helps create value for a company, but from different points of view. The functions should work together to find an optimal balance between risk and potential reward (or profit). Mutual understanding is thus essential. ARIMA graduates are awarded the academic title of "Master of Arts in Business" (MA) by the University of Applied Sciences BFI Vienna.

Graduates also have the opportunity of qualifying with a Double Degree from our university and one of its partner universities: University of Bologna (Italy), University of Economics in Katowice (Poland) and Alexandru Ioan Cuza University (Iași, Romania).

The programme lasts four semesters and is run in English as it is geared toward students wishing to expand their career prospects both locally and abroad. The programme is a part-time study programme, thereby providing an excellent opportunity for working professionals to further their studies. The second year involves an obligatory stay abroad, for example a two-week stay at one of the aforementioned partner universities.

The UAS BFI Vienna offers 25 new study places per year.

## Table of Contents



The appendices A - E are freely available to download on the product site of this book on springer.com.

## List of Figures

## List of Tables

Tables 14 to 30 are freely available to download at the product site of this book on springer.com.

## List of Abbreviations

| | |
|---|---|
| App | Appendix |
| 3M Euribor | Three month Euro interbank offered rate |
| BidAsk | Bid-ask spread |
| BPS | Basis Points |
| CDS | Credit default swap |
| CorpCDSPrem | Corporate CDS premium |
| DTCC | Depository Trust and Clearing Corporation's |
| GARCH | Generalised autoregressive conditional heteroscedasticity |
| GDP | Gross domestic product |
| GVLMA | Global validation of linear models assumptions |
| ISDA | International Swaps and Derivatives Association |
| LOVCF | Last observed value carrying forward |
| PV | Present value |
| RA | Risk Appetite |
| RFR | Risk-free rate |
| Vola | Volatility |

## Abstract

The aim of this thesis is to investigate how credit default swap spreads are impacted by an increase of government bond yields within the European area. Therefore, in the first step credit default swap spreads are modelled by the model of Hull and White in order to demonstrate the theoretical calculation of spreads. Subsequently, the relationship between government bonds and credit default swaps is displayed by the factor model of Fontana and Scheicher. Based on this model, the impact of increasing bond yields on credit default swap spreads is simulated.

The empirical analysis is based on two sample periods in order to incorporate different interest rate environments.

The findings show that frequently increasing government bond yields negatively affect credit default swap spreads. Moreover, high variation of the level of credit default swap spread changes for the various countries are given. Comparing both sample periods, commonly substantially lower credit default swap spread changes are observed within the second sample period.

# 1 Introduction

To understand and participate in the financial market a broad knowledge about the interactions between financial instruments is crucial. One can observe stronger and weaker relationships among different financial assets. These interactions can change due to the prevailing level of the financial market. Especially the financial crisis in 2007 to 2008 and its consequences as well as the European sovereign debt crisis which started in 2009 showed the impact of a changing environment and its effect on the various interactions. In addition, the prevailing low interest rate environment gives a new impetus to rethink the impact of financial instruments to one another.

Due to the tremendous current developments of the financial market, analysing the interaction between government bonds and credit derivatives depicts an excellent research field.

Government bonds of developed countries had been considered as highly secure concerning probability of default. Hence, government bonds fulfilled the assumption to be used as a good proxy for the long-term risk-free rate. As a result, important papers on sovereign credit default swaps (CDS) excluded European area countries. However, within the last decade also the probability of default of European area sovereign debt has increased.[1] Thus, the spread of government bonds should be investigated.

Within the credit derivative classes credit default swaps are chosen to be analysed since the sovereign credit default swaps market has attracted considerable attention after September 2008. In addition, within the European area one could observe substantial movements for credit default swaps spreads in recent years, as shown by Greek bonds.[2] These movements can be explained by the fact that the level and behaviour of CDS spreads have been seen as an important indicator of the economic health of a particular country.[3]

---

1 Fontana/Scheicher (2010), pp. 6-7.
2 Fontana/Scheicher (2010), p. 6.
3 Gündüz/Kaya (2014), p. 426.

Due to the development of government bonds and credit default swaps an in depth analysis of the impact of a spread change of government bonds on credit default swaps represents an important field to be addressed. Therefore, this thesis analyses whether a different degree of increase level has a different effect on the price of credit default swaps. If yes, it will be further observed how this difference changes by the varying degree of increase. In addition, the influence of the interest rate level at the beginning of the simulation will be investigated.

## 1.1 Research questions

The main research question is dedicated to the relationship between different financial assets and how these assets can impact each other. For that, the impact on the relationship between government bonds and credit default swaps are investigated:

*Which effects can be observed by a spread increase of government bonds on credit default swaps within the European area, focusing on price movements?*

Further, this thesis analysis the effects of that relationship and how the prevailing environment influences it. This will be addressed by the following two sub-questions:

*Does the impact of an increase of the spreads flatten or even diminish at a certain increase level?*

*Does the prevailing interest rate environment have a substantial effect on this impact?*

The thesis improves the existing literature in two main ways. First, the literature base for the relationship of corporate bonds to credit default swaps is by far more advanced than the relatedness between government bonds and CDS. Most prior work on CDS is based on investment-grade corporations even though the sovereign market is enormous in the sense of the volume of credit risk transfer. Sovereigns are among the largest high-yield borrowers in the world. They are characterised by more bonds outstanding, longer maturities, larger issues and more liquidity than their corporate counterparts. Moreover, there may be less information asymmetry between market participants for sovereign credit instruments compared to traders of corporate credit risk.[4] Second, the analysis focuses on government bonds in the European area and thus considers the increased probability of default of countries. Traditional government bonds issued by developed countries have been characterized by low probability of default.[5] Yet, the loss of confidence in sovereign debt markets due to the so called Eurozone sovereign debt crisis had an influence on the probability of default. This crisis has resulted in large financial interventions in Greece, Ireland and Portugal.[6]

## 1.2 Methodology

The first part of the master thesis consists of a qualitative research method based on a literature review. Thus, to give a profound knowledge base the paper starts by describing the financial assets, bonds and credit derivatives, their relationship to each other and pervious work on this subject.

The main part of the thesis is based on a quantitative research method. To depict the spread of government bonds, German government bonds are taken as a benchmark. Then the price of credit default swaps is calculated by a model, including the spread of government bonds.

To calculate the spreads of sovereign credit default swaps a structural model approach[7], arbitrage models or factor models can be applied.[8]

Within the master thesis the spread of credit default swap is calculated by the arbitrage model[9] from Hull and White as well as by the factor model

---

4 Ammer/Cai (2007), pp. 4-6.
5 Fontanta/Scheicher (2010), p. 6.
6 Calice et al. (2013), p. 122.
7 Gapen et al. (2008), pp. 109-148.
8 Meissner (2005), p. 151.
9 Hull/White (2000), pp. 2-35.

from Fontana and Scheicher.[10] The advantage of an arbitrage model is that the calculated credit default swap price approximately equals the observed price in the market. By contrast, the factor model from Fontana and Scheicher is explicitly developed for the European area. Thus, it represents an appropriate choice for the master thesis.

To answer the first research question which analyses the impact of an increase of government bond spread, a simulation is conducted. This simulation will be based on the factor model from Fontana and Scheicher. Further sub-questions are answered by adjusting the factors within the model developed by Fontana and Scheicher.

The data is taken from Bloomberg and thus is secondary data. The bond data is based on generic bond indices with a maturity of five years. Indices are chosen to ensure continuous data availability. As the bond data, the data for CDS is based on indices to ensure consecutively data availability. The maturity of the CDS indices for the model of Fontana and Scheicher is five years since these are the most liquid ones. Within the analysis German government bonds are used as benchmark. The underlying horizon for which the data is taken is a) from 2010 to 2012 and b) from 2013 to 2015. Consequently, a different underlying interest level of the data is incorporated.

The countries which represent the European area within the thesis are Belgium, Finland, France, Ireland, Italy, Netherlands, Portugal, Spain, Sweden and United Kingdom. Hence, data from ten different countries are analysed. The selection of countries ensures that stable and distressed economies are embedded in the analysis.

## 1.3 Structure

The remainder of this thesis is organised as follows. The introduction is finished with the acknowledgment of previous work. Section 2 reviews theoretical underpinnings to provide a brief overview of topics which are dealt within this thesis. Section 3 discusses the data and outlines the

10 Fontana/Scheicher (2010), pp. 15-17.

model employed, while section 4 and 5 are concerned with the simulation of government bond spread increases and the results. Section 6 offers concluding remarks.

## 1.4 Acknowledgment of previous work on the subject

Reviewing bond spreads literature, the studies of Amato and Remolona (2003) which analyse the credit spread puzzle based on corporate bonds have to be mentioned. To compute bond spreads different proxies for the risk-free interest rate can be found in the literature. Longstaff et al. (2003) use the Treasury rate as a benchmark, whereas Blanco et al. (2003) utilize the swap rate. Houweling and Vorst (2002) contribute to this research by stating that the credit default swap market appears to use the swap rate.

Within the literature on CDS, most prior work is based on corporate default swaps. Thus, this literature base is much wider compared to literature of sovereign CDS. Longstaff et al. (2005) or Blanco et al. (2005) discuss empirical comparisons of CDS and bond pricing considering investment-grade corporation. Longstaff et al. (2005) find clear evidence that the implied cost of credit protection is substantially higher in the corporate bond market, yet, wide cross-sectional variation is given. The later study reports that the corporate CDS lead the corporate bonds in determining the price of credit risk. Hull et al. (2004) investigate how credit rating announcements can influence the relationship between corporate CDS spreads and bond yields. Norden and Weber (2009) interrogate the relationship between CDS, corporate bond market and the stock market. Zhu (2006) compares credit spreads between bonds and CDS.

Nonetheless, the research for sovereign CDS enhances. Packer and Suthiphongchai (2003) investigate the growth of sovereign CDS. Rubia et al. (2016) discuss the general understanding of how CDS prices are formed, whereas Gapen et al. (2008) goes beyond that and develops a new framework to measure and analyse sovereign risk. Gracia et al. (2014) discuss the relationship between government bond spreads and

CDS premium in order to find useful tools to measure sovereign risk, based on developed and emerging economies. Pan and Singleton (2008) focus more on default and recovery which is implicitly given by the term structure of sovereign CDS spreads.

Research based on the European area has been conducted by Calica et al. (2013) which investigate liquidity spillovers in sovereign bond and CDS markets. Arce et al. (2013) examine whether sovereign CDS and bond markets reflect the same information on their prices. Furthermore, working papers by Fontana and Scheicher (2012) and Palladini and Porter (2011) discuss the relation and price dynamics of sovereign CDS and government bonds in the European area. Focusing on the impacts of the financial crisis Gündüz and Kaya (2014) analyse the persistence patterns and co-movements of sovereign CDS.

In the area for credit risk pricing two approaches dominate within literature. Structural models based on Merton (1974) and reduced-form models as discussed by Jarrow and Turnbull (1995). Important references for the first approach are Black and Cox (1976) or Longstaff and Schwartz (1995). The second approach is also discussed by Jarrow et al. (1997) and Duffie and Singleton (1999). Both approaches are examined in detail by Lando (1997) and Schönbucher (2000).

Arbitrage-free models are another important approach within the valuation of credit risk. Main reference for that are the studies of Hull and White (2000a, 2000b). Within the literature, arbitrage-free models may be counted to reduced-form models.[11]

[11] Blanco et al. (2005), p. 2258.

# 2 Theoretical underpinnings

The following section gives a brief overview of the topics which are dealt in this thesis. Thus the financial assets, bonds and credit defaults swaps are discussed. Further, spreads within the financial market and the theoretical relationship between bonds and CDS are reviewed. Models used to price CDS conclude this chapter.

## 2.1 Bonds

Bonds are the securitised version of loans and are referred to as fixed income products. They are tradeable in small denominations and their major important identifying properties are a) its issuer, b) the maturity c) the coupon and the coupon's frequency.

Based on the issuer, one can distinguish between corporate and government bonds. Whereas corporate bonds are issued by companies to increase financing, government bonds are issued by sovereign governments, states or municipalities.

In addition, bonds can be classified based on their maturity into a) short-term, b) mid-term or c) long-term bonds. Short-term bonds usually mature within three years, mid-term bonds between three to seven years and long-term bonds in more than seven years.

The third major identifying property of bonds, the coupon size, is commonly expressed as a percentage of the nominal amount. Commonly it will be distributed on an annually, semi-annually or quarterly basis. Determining the coupon payment, principles like the day-count convention or day-shift convention have to be considered, especially if the coupon payment date falls on a holiday. Bonds based on different coupon types might be a zero-coupon bond, fixed-coupon bond or a par floater.

The simplest form of a bond is a zero-coupon bond. A bond of such type is issued at a considerable discount to the par value. Yet, as the name implies no coupon will be paid out. Fixed-coupon bonds distribute their coupons on a fixed basis stipulated in advance and one usually assumes that the notional amount is repaid at maturity. The coupon amounts of a par floater are linked to a benchmark interest rate augmented by a constant spread. At maturity a par floater will pay out the principal.

Government bonds are distinguished based on their maturity into a) Treasury bills, b) Treasury notes and c) Treasury bonds. Whereas bills classify government debt issued for less than one year, notes mature within one to ten years. Bonds mature in more than ten years.

Moreover, government bonds can be further distinguished based on their terminology affected by the country of issue. Thus, the terms Treasury bills, notes or bonds are usually used in the United States of America, whereas in Great Britain government bonds are usually called Gilts. In Germany government bonds are denominated as Bunds.

Based on the coupon frequency, bonds issued by the United States of America are commonly characterized by a semi-annual coupon payment, whereas annual coupons are common for European bonds.

The issuer rating also plays a major role for the risk premium and thus for the pricing of the bond. However, ratings affect corporate bonds in terms of pricing even more than government bonds.

Corporate bonds usually offer a higher yield than government bonds due to higher default rates for companies reflected by the rating of the issuing entity.

Compared to government bonds, corporate bonds can have more additional features. Thus, they may be convertible bonds or callable bonds. Convertible bonds enable the holder of the bond in question to convert the bond into shares of the company that issued this particular bond. Callable bonds can be redeemed earlier by the issuer. Therefore, the holder of the bond usually receives a higher yield. [12]

## 2.2 Credit derivatives

The term credit derivatives covers a broad scope of derivative securities. According to Schönbuchner two definitions can be used to determine

[12] Schönbuchner (2003), pp. 11-12.

credit derivatives. Both definitions are based on credit risk which is defined as the risk that an obligor does not honour its obligation.

The first definition is given by:

*" a) A credit derivative is a derivative security that is primarily used to transfer, hedge or manage credit risk.*

*b) A credit derivative is a derivative security whose payoff is materially affected by credit risk."*[13]

The second definition states:

*"A credit derivative is a derivative security that has a payoff which is conditioned on the occurrence of a credit event. The credit event is defined with respect to a reference credit (or several reference credits), and the reference credit asset(s) issued by the reference credit. If the credit event has occurred, the default payment has to be made by one of the counterparties.*

*Besides the default payment a credit derivative can have further payoffs that are not default contingent."*[14]

The first definition classifies a derivative as a credit derivative based on the intended use. As this definition is applied on a broader scope, forwards and options on defaultable bonds, total return swaps on defaultable bonds, credit spreads options or credit default swaps are covered.

The second definition is applied on derivatives that focus mainly on credit risk. Hence the credit risk is isolated. Instruments covered by this definition would be credit default swaps, basket credit derivatives or similar products.[15]

---

[13] Schönbuchner (2003), p.8.
[14] Schönbuchner (2003), p.8.
[15] Schönbuchner (2003), pp.1-8.

Key credit derivatives are asset swaps, total return swaps, collateralized debt obligations, spread options and credit default swaps.

Asset swaps are in general used to transform an investor's asset characteristics. Thus, the fixed coupon payments of a defaultable bond, which represents the asset, might be replaced by a payoff stream of Libor plus a spread by using an interest-rate swap.[16]

A total return swap replaces the actual return of one asset by the return of another one. Since usually one of these assets will be a defaultable asset like a bond and the other one a riskless asset like Libor they will mainly differ in terms of credit risk and thus the total return swap is classified as credit derivative.[17]

Collateralized debt obligations are financial instruments to securitise a portfolio of defaultable assets like bonds, loans or credit default swaps. The assets are sold to a special purpose vehicle which has been specially created for that purpose. Subsequently the debt obligations will be allocated to tranches and sold to investors. The obligations are collateralized by the underlying assets.[18]

Spread options imply the right to trade bonds at given spreads exceeding a reference yield.[19]

### *2.2.1 Credit default swaps*

Credit default swaps represent one of the most important financial assets within credit derivatives. Hence CDSs account for a major portion of the credit derivative market. Moreover, due to their liquidity compared to other credit derivatives they form the basic building blocks for more complex structured credit products.[20]

The second definition of credit derivatives defined by Schönbuchner states important characteristics of credit default swaps which are financial

16 Schönbuchner (2003), p. 12.
17 Duffie (1998), p. 2.
18 Schönbuchner (2003), p. 46.
19 Duffie (1998), p. 2.
20 Blanco et al. (2005), p. 2256.

assets that transfer the credit risk. Therefore, two parties enter into a contractual agreement that provides protection against the risk of a credit event occurring by a reference entity. The first party, the buyer of protection against default, wants to be insured against the possibility of default on a reference asset (reference credit asset) issued by a reference entity (reference credit). The second party, the seller of protection against default, is willing to bear the risk associated with the default of the reference entity. The reference credit might be a particular company or country. The reference asset usually refers to a bond issued by the reference entity.

The agreement can be seen as an insurance policy.[21] Therefore, the protection buyer refers to the insured counterparty and the seller to the insurer.[22]

According to the agreement the insured counterparty makes a periodical or upfront payment (credit default swap premium/ credit default swap spread) to the insurer[23] that is typically defined as a per annum rate in basis points of the notional. As outlined in the agreement, the payment will be paid until the maturity date of the contract or the credit event occurs.[24] As consideration, the insurer promises to make a payment if the credit event takes place (default payment). This can be either done through a physical or cash settlement. A physical settlement describes the repayment at par against physical delivery of a reference asset. By contrast, a cash settlement is defined as the payment of the notional amount minus the post-default market value of the reference asset[25], or a predetermined fraction of the notional.[26]

Credit events defined by the International Swaps and Derivatives Association (hereinafter referred to as ISDA) are a) bankruptcy, b) failure to payment, c) obligation default or acceleration, d) repudiation or moratorium or e) restructuring.[27] Whereas bankruptcy refers to the reference

21 Duffie (1999), p. 74
22 Longstaff et al. (2003), p.4.
23 Alexopoulou et al. (2009), p.6.
24 Ammer/ Cai (2007), pp. 3-4.
25 Blanco et al. (2005), p. 2257.
26 Longstaff et al. (2003), p. 5.
27 Blanco et al. (2005), p. 2257.

entity itself, the other standardised credit events are defined with respect to the reference obligation. Given the standardised credit events, CDS agreements might also state other events that trigger default. Consequently the buyer and a seller of protection against default might agree on a credit event that differs from the standardised events defined by ISDA. However, the majority of traded CDS are according to the specifications which have been proposed by the ISDA.[28]

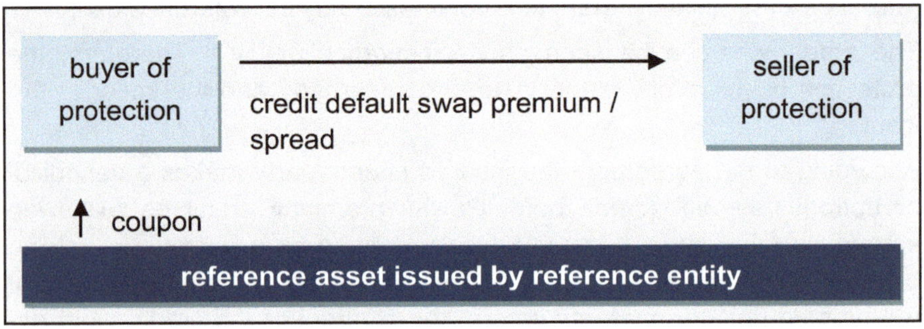


**Figure 1** Payments within a CDS agreement

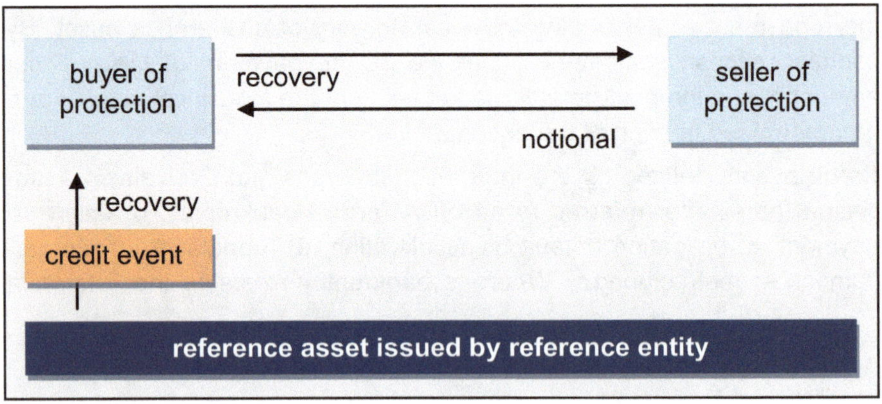


**Figure 2** Payments within a CDS agreement when credit event occurred

[28] Schönbuchner (2003), pp. 9-15.

To determine a CDS one has to know 1) the reference obligor and his reference assets, 2) the definition of the credit event that is to be insured, 3) the notional of the CDS, 4) the start of the CDS and thus the start of the protection, 5) the maturity date, 6) the credit default swap spread, 7) the frequency and day-count convention for the spread payments and 8) the payment at the credit event and its settlement.[29]

Moreover, specific arrangements can be stipulated in the CDS contract. The most important specifications are concerned with accrual payments and delivery options. Accrual payments refer to the payment the protection buyer is required to pay if the CDS arrangement stipulates periodic payments and the credit event occurs. Delivery options refer to the fact that in case of physical settlement the buyer may choose from a list of obligations which are similar to the reference obligation.[30]

If the credit event is based on the default of one single obligor, the CDS refers to a single-name credit default swap. These credit derivatives are used to manage individual exposure concentrations. However, to manage the default risk on a portfolio basis, basket and portfolio credit derivatives are used like first-to-default swaps or basket default swaps.[31]

## 2.3 Spreads in general

Within finance one frequently has to deal with spreads. A spread is defined as the differential between two economically comparable variables which are of the same unity. Depending on the context, the spread may be classified as price-related, interest-related or related to forward transactions.

Price-related spreads cover the well-known bid-ask spread as well as the spread between spot and forward prices within exchange transactions.

---

29 Schönbuchner (2003), pp. 15-16.
30 Houweling/Vorst (2005), p. 1202.
31 Schönbuchner (2003), p. 43.

Interest-related spreads refer to the yield differentials/ yield spreads, yet may also refer to credit spreads. Yield differentials may either represent the differential between short-term and long-term interest rates or the spread between a bond and a comparable risk-free bond.[32] Credit spreads are also classified as interest-related spreads since they represent the spread resulting from the comparison of bonds with similar maturity, yet different credit quality.[33]

Yield differentials represent important indicators for the market perceptions of fiscal vulnerability which causes an adjustment of the market discipline on national governments' fiscal policies. Even small yield differentials may lead to a substantial impact in countries where debt already exceeds the gross domestic product.[34]

The yield differentials are determined by liquidity and credit default risk. Bonds which can be traded immediately at low transaction costs even in an adverse market environment will be offered at lower yields than less liquid bonds. Nevertheless, the yield differential increases when the probability that the issuer of the bond may not honour the obligation in full augments. Moreover, empirical research has shown that also international risk affects yield differentials.[35]

Spreads that are related to forward transactions refer inter alia to options strategies like bull spreads or bear spreads.[36]

Besides the above mentioned main types of spreads others like the credit default swap spread, which represents the cost per annum for protection against a default by a company/ government or the asset swap spread are existing. Due to the definition, however, one can classify this kind of spread as a price-related spread.

---

32 Fontana/Scheicher (2010), pp. 5-7.
33 Amato/Remolona (2003), p. 51.
34 Codogno et al. (2003), pp. 506-514.
35 Codogno et al. (2003), pp. 506-514.
36 Hull (2012), pp. 238-249.

## 2.4 Relationship between bond yield differentials and credit default swaps spreads

Due to the arbitrage argument, bond yield differentials and CDS spreads should be closely related in theory. Therefore, the cash flows from a portfolio consisting of a par yield bond issued by the reference entity with a maturity of n-years and a credit default swap with a maturity of n-years should be similar to the cash flows of a par yield riskless bond with a maturity of n-years in all states of the world. The yield relationship between the assets should thus be approximately

$$s = y - r \tag{1}$$

where $s$ denotes the CDS spread with a maturity of n-year, $y$ defines the yield of a par yield bond issued by the reference entity with a maturity of n-years and $r$ denotes the yield on a par yield riskless bond with maturity of n-years.

As a result of the arbitrage argument, an arbitrageur would purchase a riskless bond and sell a par yield bond of a reference entity as well as the credit default swap in the case of $s$ being greater than $y - r$. Conversely, if $s$ would be less than $y - r$, the arbitrageur would purchase a par yield bond of a reference entity as well as the credit default swap and sell the riskless bond.

However, this arbitrage argument is subject to a number of assumptions and approximations. First, short selling of par yield bonds of a reference entity is possible by market participants. In addition, it is assumed that selling bonds of a reference entity as well as the credit default swap and purchasing riskless bonds is possible when $s$ is greater than $y - r$. Second, short selling of riskless bonds is possible by market participants which is equivalent to assume that borrowing at the riskless rate is possible for market participants. Third, the cheapest-to-deliver-option which is given for credit default swaps is ignored. Thus, in the case of credit event, the protection seller can choose which bond will be delivered as long as certain characteristics are met. Fourth, constant interest rates are assumed and thus par yield bond would remain par yield bonds. Fifth, counterparty default risk is given within the credit default swap. Sixth, precise definition of credit event and thus circumstances when default payments are done based on the ISDA documentation. Seventh, due to tax and liquidity reasons an investor prefers a riskless bond rather than a par yield bond of a reference entity and a credit default swap or vice versa. Finally, credit default swaps imply the right to sell the par yield bond of a reference entity for its face value augmented by accrued interest. However, in practice credit default swaps imply the right to sell a bond for its face value.

The relationship between a credit default swap with a maturity of n-years, a par yield bond issued by the reference entity with a maturity of n-years and a par yield riskless bond with a maturity of n-years can be adjusted to account for the last assumption. Therefore the above mentioned equation (1) would be adapted as following

$$s = \frac{y - r}{1 + A^*} \tag{2}$$

where $A^*$ is defined as the expected accrued interest on the par yield bond issued by the reference entity at the time of default.[37]

The same can be expressed with regards to the basis. The basis is defined by the difference between the CDS spread and the bond yield differential based on the same reference entity, with the yield differential determined by the difference between a risky bond and a risk-free bond with the same maturity. Assuming perfect arbitrage among the cash and synthetic market, the basis should be equal to zero at equilibrium

$$BASIS = s - (y - r) = 0 \tag{3}$$

In order to prove the theoretical arbitrage argument, each characteristic of the two bonds must be the same. Moreover, the counterparty risk related to the credit default swap must be neglected.

37 Hull et al. (2004), pp. 2794-2795.

In addition, numerous other non-fundamental factors may influence the CDS prices. The most important factors are liquidity premium, rating agencies perspectives and speculative predatory behaviour. To provide an accurate presentation of the theoretical interrelation between bond and CDS prices each impact caused by a substantial common factor that affects this relationship has to be balanced.

The basis can be either positive or negative prior to the expiration. In the case of a fixed-coupon bond hedged by a CDS, the basis would increase when the spot price increases by more than the CDS price. As a result, the basis would turn positive if the risk premium on a defaultable bond is too low or the CDS spread is too high. The basis can return to its equilibrium value of zero by selling the defaultable bond, however, due to the inelasticity of the cash market it may be that the basis remains positive. By contrast, the basis would decrease when the CDS price rises by more than the spot price. Subsequently, a negative basis would be given if the risk premium on a defaultable bond is larger than its theoretical value or the CDS spread is too low. In order that the basis returns to zero the riskless bond has to be sold.

To satisfy the arbitrage argument, the basis would be sold if it is positive. The profit arising from this trade results from the enhanced credit quality of the reference entity which would not causes default payments that have to be paid out. On the contrary, the basis would be bought if it is negative. In this case the profit arises from the worsening of the credit quality of the reference entity.

The basis is determined by various factors. First, usually CDS premiums are always positive resulting from the fixed payment to the protection seller. Even for bonds that have a low probability of default the protection seller expects a positive CDS premium in order to write the protection. Thus the basis may be positively biased. Second, the cheapest-to-deliver-option embedded in the CDS might influence especially CDS that are settled physically. Third, the accrued coupon on the defaultable bond that will be delivered to the protection buyer in case of default if stipulated may have a positive impact on the basis. Fourth, the basis may be positively affected by a reference bond of a CDS trading below par when the credit event occurs. Thus, the protection seller experiences a higher loss than an investor holding the asset in terms of cash. Fifth, an additional premium may be charged for illiquid market segments which drives the basis upwards. However, if the defaultable bond market is less liquid than the riskless bond market which may lead to a yield differential increase, the basis would be affected negatively. Finally the counterparty risk taken on by the protection buyer as well as the counterparty risk to which the protection seller is exposed influence the basis.

In general, factors that have a greater impact on the risk profile of the CDS tend to raise the basis, whereas factors influencing the creditworthiness of the bond relative to the CDS decrease the basis. Factors that may raise the bond return relative to the CDS increase the basis. However, they equally decrease the basis if the relative return to the CDS increases.[38]

## 2.5 Models for pricing CDSs

To price CDSs two main approaches can be distinguished which are the structural model approach and the reduced-form model. In addition, factor models may be used to price CDSs.

### *2.5.1 Structural model approach*

First, a structural model, based on Merton (1974), can be used to determine credit spreads. Therefore, the liabilities of a reference entity are comprised of equity and debt. The equity value is modelled as a European call option on the assets value and the debt value is determined by the difference between a riskless debt and a European put option on the assets value. It is assumed that the reference entity's assets follow a geometric Brownian motion. Default occurs when the assets' value falls below the debts' nominal at a particular time point.

The model assumes further frictionless markets, borrowing and lending is possible at the same constant riskless short rate, assets can be traded

38 Palladini/Portes (2011), pp. 5-13.

continuously, short-selling is unlimited, no dividend payments and no new debt is issued and information regarding asset value is given.

Based on this approach, credit spread is determined by the difference between continuously compounded yields-to-maturity, also called spot rates, of the defaultable and riskless zero-coupon bond. Thus the credit spread $S_{(t,T)}$ is given by

$$S_{(t,T)} = -\frac{1}{T-t} \ln \left( N(d_{t,2}) + \frac{V_t}{De^{-r(T-t)}} N(-d_{t,1}) \right) \tag{4}$$

$$d_{t,1} = \frac{\ln\left(\frac{V_t}{D}\right) + \left(r + \frac{\sigma_V^2}{2}\right)(T-t)}{\sigma_V \sqrt{T-t}} \tag{5}$$

$$d_{t,2} = d_{t,1} - \sigma_v \sqrt{T-t} \tag{6}$$

where $V_t$ represents the assets' value, $D$ defines the debt value, $r$ describes the riskless rate, $\sigma_V$ denotes the variance of the assets, $t$ defines the valuation date and $T$ represents the maturity. [39]

However, this model has several disadvantages as it is based only on one reference entity, complete information regarding this reference entity is needed and default only takes place at a discrete time point. Therefore, numerous extensions of the original structural model have been provided.

### 2.5.2 Reduced-form models

Second, a reduced-form model, also known as intensity model can be used. Within this model default is determined as a random time point with a stochastic arrival intensity. The credit spread is defined by risk neutral

[39] Merton (1974), pp. 449-469.

valuation without arbitrage opportunities.[40] Hence, a reduced-form model may also refer to as arbitrage model.

To calculate a CDS spread using an intensity model, several assumptions have to be made. At time $t$, all prices of defaultable and riskless zero-coupon bonds are known for maturities $T \geq t$. Furthermore, bond prices are characterised by absence of arbitrage and defaultable zero-coupon bonds have a recovery of zero at default. In addition, the time of default is independent of the riskless interest-rate given pricing probabilities. Finally, analysis are done within the risk-neutral probability measure $Q$.

The model is based on the riskless discount factors, defaultable discount factors with zero recovery and the conditional defaultable discount factors. These building factors are determined by the riskless forward rates, the hazard rate at default and the expected recovery rate. The forward rates and the hazard rates can be specified by parametric forms which may be a step function like a poisson process, polynomial function or cubic splines.

In order to obtain the equation to model a bond price and a CDS price the following definitions have to be made:

A riskless zero-coupon bond pays off one at maturity $T$ in every state of the world. By contrast, a defaultable zero-coupon bond pays off one at maturity only if the credit event did not occur until $T$. Since the time of default is independent of the riskless interest rate under the risk-neutral probability measure, following holds:

$$P^*(t,T) = P(t,T)Q(t,T) \tag{7}$$

where $P^*(t,T)$ denotes the price at time $t$ of a defaultable zero-coupon bond paying one at time $T$ if $\tau > T$, $P(t,T)$refers to the price at time $t$ of a zero-coupon bond paying off one at time $T$, $Q(t,T)$defines the implied probability of survival over $[t,T]$ and

$\tau$ denoting the time of default.

---

[40] Zhu (2006), p. 214.

Given the equation above, the implied survival probability is the ratio of the defaultable and riskless zero-coupon bond prices

$$Q(t,T) = \frac{P^*(t,T)}{P(t,T)} \tag{8}$$

The implied survival probability is a non-negative decreasing function of the maturity which equals one at initiation.

The complementary to the implied survival probability is given by the implied default probability $Q^{def}(t,T)$ which is determined by

$$Q^{def}(t,T) = 1 - Q(t,T) \tag{9}$$

However, the implied survival probability has certain disadvantages. First, cumulative probabilities are overlapping within time intervals which means that both $P(t,T_1)$ and $P(t,T_2)$ relate to the default risk in $[t,T_1]$. Second, implied survival probabilities are affected by the length of the time interval. Hence, survival probabilities of a longer maturity are more sensitive than survival probabilities of a shorter maturity. To overcome the first disadvantage conditional survival probabilities are used:

$$Q(t,T_1,T_2) = \frac{Q(t,T_2)}{Q(t,T_1)} \tag{10}$$

It follows that the survival probability until $T_2$ equals the survival probability until $T_1$ multiplied by the survival probability from $T_1$ to $T_2$, given survival until $T_1$:

$$Q(t,T_2) = Q(t,T_1)Q(t,T_1,T_2) \tag{11}$$

The second drawback of implied survival probabilities still remains for conditional survival probability. Thus, default probabilities per a certain length of time interval referring to as implied hazard rates are used.

The implied discrete hazard rate of default over $[T, T+\Delta t]$ as seen from time $t$ is given by

$$H(t,T,T+\Delta t) := \frac{1}{\Delta t}\left(\frac{Q(t,T)}{Q(t,T+\Delta t} - 1\right) \tag{12}$$

The implied instantaneous hazard rate of default for time $T$ as seen from time $t$ is given by

$$h(t,T) := \lim_{\Delta t \to 0} H(t,T,T+\Delta t) \tag{13}$$

The implied instantaneous hazard rate of default can also be expressed in terms of the spread of defaultable and riskless continuously compounded forward rates as seen from time $t$

$$h(t,T) = f^*(t,T) - f(t,T) \tag{14}$$

where$f^*(t,T)$ defines the defaultable riskless instantaneous continuously compounded forward rate for $T$ as seen from $t$ and $f(t,T)$ denotes the riskless instantaneous continuously compounded forward rate for $T$ as seen from $t$.

It can be said that within a short time interval $[T, T+\Delta t]$ the default probability is approximately proportional to the interval length $\Delta t$ with the short-term credit spread as proportional factor.

$$Q^{def}(t,t,t+\Delta t) \approx \left(r^*(t) - r(t)\right) * \Delta t = \lambda(t) * \Delta t \tag{15}$$

Where $r^*(t)$ is equal to $f^*(t,t)$ and $r(t)$ is equal to $f(t,t)$.

Specifying the building blocks of the model, the riskless discount factors are determined by

$$P(0,t_k) = \prod_{j=1}^{k} \frac{1}{1+\delta_j F(0,t_{j-1},t_j)} \tag{16}$$

where $\delta$ refers to the day-count fraction between time points and $F$ determines the simply compounded forward rate.

The defaultable discount factors with zero recovery is given by

$$P^*(0,t_k) = P(0,t_k)\prod_{j=1}^{k}\frac{1}{1+\delta_j H(0,t_{j-1},t_j)} \tag{17}$$

and the conditional defaultable discount factors by

$$E(0,t_{k-1},t_k) = \delta_k P^*(0,t_k)H(0,t_{k-1},t_k) \tag{18}$$

Applying the above mentioned definitions and the building blocks, the price of a defaultable fix-coupon bond within a reduced-form model would be determined by

$$B_{fix}(0) = c^*\sum_{n=1}^{N}\Delta_n P^*(0,T_n) + P^*(0,T_N) + \pi\sum_{k=1}^{K}E(0,t_{k-1},t_k) \tag{19}$$

where $c^*$ describes the coupon payments and $\pi$ represents the expected recovery rate.

The price of a defaultable bond with variable coupons would be determined by

$$\begin{aligned} B_{var}(0) = &\sum_{n=1}^{N}\Delta_n F(0,T_{n-1},T_n)P^*(0,T_n) + s^*\sum_{n=1}^{N}\Delta_n P^*(0,T_n) \\ &+ P^*(0,T_n) + \pi\sum_{k=1}^{K}E(0,t_{k-1},t_k) \end{aligned} \tag{20}$$

where $s^*$ denotes the spread over Libor per annum in percentage.[41]

[41] Schönbuchner (2003), pp. 52-67.

The price of a CDS can be determined based on its fixed and floating leg payment. The fixed payment leg denotes the protection payment to the protection seller and is given[42], neglecting accrued premiums, by[43]

$$PV_{fix}(0) = s^*(0) \sum_{n=1}^{N} \Delta_n P^*(0, T_n) \tag{21}$$

The floating leg represents the payment of the protection seller to the protection buyer in case the credit event occurs[44] and is given by

$$PV_{def}(0) = (1 - \pi) \sum_{k=1}^{K} E(0, t_{k-1}, t_k) \tag{22}$$

Thus, balancing the two legs, the CDS price at inception is obtained by

$$s^*(0) = (1 - \pi) \frac{\sum_{k=1}^{K} E(0, t_{k-1}, t_k)}{\sum_{n=1}^{N} \Delta_n P^*(0, T_n)} \tag{23}$$

After initiation, the mark-to-market value of a CDS will equal to

$$MtM(t) = (s^*(t) - s^*(0)) \sum_{n=1}^{N} \Delta_n P^*(t, T_n) \tag{24}$$

Reduced-form models are based on the work from Jarrow and Turnbull (1995) or Duffie and Singleton (1999). These models have been further developed. Thus, numerous extensions of the above mentioned simple intensity models can be found in the literature.[45]

---

42 Houweling/Vorst (2005), p. 1205.
43 Schönbuchner (2003), p. 67.
44 Houweling/Vorst (2005), p. 1205.
45 Schönbuchner (2003), pp. 67-68.

### 2.5.3 Factor models

Factor analysis are statistical methods which determine a dependent variable as a combination of potential explanatory variables referred to as factors. Thus, the model analysis the dependence between variables.[46]

Linear regression can be used if the dependency is modelled linear. Thus, the dependent variable is determined as a linear combination of the explanatory variables plus an error term.

$$y = \beta_0 + \beta_1 x_1 + \beta_2 x_2 + \cdots \ldots + \beta_n x_n + \epsilon \quad (25)$$

Standard linear regression models assume linearity, independence, homoscedasticity and normality. Thus a linear relationship between the depended and explanatory variable should be given, applying a linear regression model. Furthermore, observations are independent and the variables have the same variance. Finally, the dependent variable alter normal around its mean.

In addition, a lack of multicollinearity must be given for multiple linear regression models. Multicollinearity refers to the circumstance that explanatory variables may have a higher degree of correlation between themselves.[47]

Regression can also be applied on other than linear relationships. However, more advance regression methods are used.

46 Fontana/Scheicher (2010), p. 15.
47 Carol (2008), pp. 144-146.

# 3 Modelling credit default swap prices

The following section describes the chosen models and the needed data in order to guarantee a successful implementation. At the end of this section, the programming of the models and its resulting parameters and outcomes are discussed.

## 3.1 Classification of models

This section discusses the two selected models, which are the reduced-form model by Hull and White and the factor model by Fontana and Scheicher.

### *3.1.1 Hull and White model*

The arbitrage-free model developed by Hull and White in 2000 aims to value CDSs under the condition that the payoff depends on default by a single reference entity excluding counterparty default risk. Therefore, the risk-neutral probability of the reference entity at different time points has to be estimated first. The model calculates its estimates based on the following relationship where the value of Treasury bond represents the benchmark of zero-default-risk rates and assumptions about recovery rates of the reference entity are incorporated:

$$\begin{aligned} &Value\ of\ treasury\ bond - Value\ of\ sovereign\ bond \\ &\qquad = PV\ of\ cost\ of\ defaults \end{aligned} \tag{26}$$

It is assumed that a set of $N$ bonds has been chosen with maturity of the $i$th bond being $t_i$with $t_1 < t_2 < \cdots < t_N$. The interest rates are constant, claim amounts are known and recovery rates are known. Furthermore, it is concluded that the claim amount equals the non-default value of the bond at default time as well as the face value plus accrued interest at default time. In addition, the model assumes that the credit event can happen at any maturity dates of the bonds, at discrete time.

In order to calculate the probability of default according to the model of Hull and White following definitions are needed:

$B_j$: Price of the $j$th bond today

$G_j$: Price of the $j$th bond today if no probability of default is given

$F_j(t)$: Forward price of the $i$th bond for a contract maturing at time $t$ and assuming that the bond is default-free $(t < t_j)$

$v(t)$: Present value of €1 received at time $t$ with certainty

$C_j(t)$: Claim of the $j$th bond by holders if default occurs at time $t$ $(t < t_j)$

$R_j(t)$: Recovery rate of the $j$th bond for holders in the credit event at time $t$ $(t < t_j)$

$a_{ij}$: Present value of the loss, relative to the value the bond would have if there were no possibility of default, form a default on the $i$th bond at time $t_i$

$p_i$: Risk-neutral probability of default at time $t$

As it is assumed that the interest rates are constant, the non-default value of the $j$th bond is given by $F_j(t)$. In case of default at time $t$, a payment which equals the recovery rate $R_j(t)$ on the claim $C_j(t)$ will be made. Hence it follows that

$$a_{ij} = v(t_i)\left[F_j(t_i) - R_j(t_i)C_j(t_i)\right] \tag{27}$$

where the loss $a_{ij}$ may occur with the probability $p_i$. As the total present value of the loss on the $j$th bond would be given by the difference between $G_j$ minus $B_j$ it follows that $p_j$ is determined by

$$p_j = \frac{G_j - B_j - \sum_{i=1}^{j-1} p_i a_{ij}}{a_{jj}} \tag{28}$$

Having determined the estimates for the probability of defaults, the valuation of the credit default swap can be conducted. Therefore, the assumptions about credit default events, interest rates and recovery rates are still valid.

Following definitions are used in order to valuate CDS according to the reduced-form model from Hull and White:

$T$: Life of CDS

$q(t)$: Risk-neutral default probability at time $t$

$R$: Expected recovery rate of the reference debt in a risk-neutral world

$u(t)$: Present value of payments at the rate of €1 per annum on payment dates between $t_0$ and $t$

$e(t)$: Present value of accrual interest at time $t$ equal to $t - t^*$ where $t^*$ represents the payment date immediately preceding $t$

$v(t)$: Present value of €1 received at time $t$

$w$: Total payments of the CDS buyer per annum

$s$: Value of $w$ that causes the CDS to be zero

$\pi$: Risk-neutral probability of no default during the life of the CDS

$A(t)$: Accrued interest of the reference debt at time $t$ as a percentage of nominal

At discrete times, if the credit event occurs the present value of payments will be $wu(T)$. If default is assumed to may happen also at time $(t < T)$, the present value of payments would equal $w[u(t) + e(t)]$ if the credit event occurs. Hence the expected present value of payments equals

$$w \int_0^T q(t)[u(t) + e(t)]dt + w\pi u(T) \tag{29}$$

Based on the assumptions about the claim amount the risk-neutral expected payoff from the credit default swaps will be given by

$$1 - [1 + A(t)]R = 1 - R - A(t)R \tag{30}$$

Hence the present value of the expected payoff from the CDS is

$$\int_0^T [1 - R - A(t)R]q(t)v(t)dt \tag{31}$$

The value of the expected payoff from the CDS minus the present value of the payments made by the buyer thus gives the value of the CDS to the buyer:

$$\int_0^T [1 - R - A(t)R]q(t)v(t)dt \\ - w\int_0^T q(t)[u(t) + e(t)]dt - w\pi u(T) \tag{32}$$

Thus the CDS spread is given by[48]

$$s = \frac{\int_0^T [1 - R - A(t)R]q(t)v(t)dt}{\int_0^T q(t)[u(t) + e(t)]dt - \pi u(T)} \tag{33}$$

### *3.1.2 Fontana and Scheicher model*

The model developed by Fontana and Scheicher in 2010 investigates whether the same factors can be used to price CDS and bond spreads. Thus the model is based on various explanatory factors which are used to calculate both spreads. In order to obtain the beta values for the model a multiple regression methodology is applied.

The choice of the factors for this model has been based inter alia on the studies of Merton (1974), Gapen et al. (2005),Hull et al. (2005), Campbell and Taksler (2003) and Tang and Yan (2007).

The model consists of six main explanatory variables which are the a) risk-free rate, b) risk appetite, c) corporate CDS premium, d) proxy for a

---

[48] Hull/White (2000), pp. 2-14.

country's public debt, e) idiosyncratic equity volatility and f) bid-ask spread.

The first factor within the model is the risk-free rate. Since this variable is negatively related to credit spreads, an increase of the risk-free rate causes a decrease of the present value of expected future cash flows. Moreover, an increase of the expected growth rate of a firm is more likely which triggers a higher firm value. As a result the credit spread should decrease by these two effects.

The second factor, the risk appetite, represents the fact that spreads may change based on changes in the risk aversion of investors even if underlying fundaments remain the same. This can be explained as the spread compensates investors for more than only the pure expected loss. Within the paper a volatility index minus a GARCH-based estimate of volatility is used for this variable. However, since this estimate is not further determined within the paper it will not be incorporate within the model. Thus the risk appetite will be represented solely by the volatility index.

Furthermore, as the credit spread incorporate more than only the expected loss, the model includes a measure of the aggregated credit market developments. Hence, the third factor is the corporate credit default swap premium represented by the iTraxx Main Investment Grade index.[49]

The fourth factor is given by a proxy of the public debt of a country. The importance of this factor is given by the fact that the leverage of a firm within structural models of sovereign credit risk has been proven to be a major risk factor.[50] It is expected that a higher debt level leads to more changes in CDS spreads. Regarding the bond market this factor reflects the bond market liquidity since a larger bond market generally contributes to market efficiency causing lower transaction costs. Yet, if overall supply exceeds existing demand an adverse effect on the bond market liquidity is likely. For bond spreads the second effect is primarily expected to be relevant. Within the model of Fontana and Scheicher a linear interpolation of the country's total outstanding bonds over the country's gross domestic

49 Fontana/Scheicher (2010), pp. 15-16.
50 Gapen et al, (2008), pp. 112-146

product is used, since the data is only available on a monthly basis. However, to be consistent within the model and its used data, this thesis will apply inter alia for this factor the last observation carrying forward (LOVCF) method.

Furthermore, the structural models of sovereign credit risk identify the volatility of sovereign assets as a major factor in order to determine the default risk of a country. Therefore, the model uses the idiosyncratic volatility. It is expected that a higher volatility level increases changes of spreads.

Finally, the sixth factor within the model is given by the bid-ask spread which is significantly positive related to credit default swap spreads. The model of Fontana and Scheicher uses therefore the same data as already used for the corporate CDS premium due to the lack of reliable data on issuer-specific sovereign CDS market liquidity. Whereas the corporate CDS premium depicts the mid price of the bid and ask price of the iTraxx Main Investment Grade, the bid-ask spread represents the difference between the two price quotes. Thus, even though the two factors are based on the same index, they represent different characteristics of the time series. Hence, confirmed by the low correlation of 14.83% for the first sample period and -9.74% for the second sample period the dependence between the two factors are inferior. Thus, the model will include all six main factors as given within the original model of Fontana and Scheicher.

Calculating the CDS and bond spreads Fontana and Scheicher use further variables, so called dummy variables. However, these dummy variables for volatility, debt, risk-free rate, risk appetite, corporate CDS premium and bid-ask spread are not explained within the paper. Hence, these variables cannot be incorporated within the model.

As a result, the adapted model of Fontana and Scheicher used to calculate CDS or bond spreads within this thesis will be as following:[51]

[51] Fontana/Scheicher (2010), pp. 16-40.

$$CDS\ spread = C + \beta_0 Risk\ free\ rate + \beta_1 Risk\ Appetite + \beta_2 Corporate\ CDS\ premium + \beta_3 Debt + \beta_4\ Volatility + \beta_5\ BidAsk\ spread + \varepsilon \quad (34)$$

$$Bond\ spread = C + \beta_0 Risk\ free\ rate + \beta_1 Risk\ Appetite + \beta_2 Corporate\ CDS\ premium + \beta_3 Debt + \beta_4\ Volatility + \beta_5\ BidAsk\ spread + \varepsilon \quad (35)$$

## 3.2 Classification of data

In order to conduct both, the arbitrage model by Hull and White and the factor model by Fontana and Scheicher two data sets are needed. The first data set used for the arbitrage model consists of bond data and the prevailing interest rate. The second data set used for the factor model incorporates data for the six risk factors besides the CDS data and bond data which are needed to estimate the beta values of the model. The data is taken from Bloomberg and thus represents secondary data. The currency of the data is Euro.

Initially, the data covered a time horizon from 2004 to 2015. Hence three sample periods from a) 1st of January 2004 to 31th of December 2006, b) 1st of January 2010 to 31th of December 2012 and c) 1st of January 2013 to 31th of December 2015 would have been used. However, since data for the CDS indices is not available before 2008 or in the case of Spain before 2009, the first sample period has been deleted.

Thus, the data chosen for this thesis cover a five year time horizon from 2010 to 2015. The sample period is chosen from a) 1st January 2010 to 31th of December 2012 and b) 1st of January 2013 to 31th of December 2015.

The following graph depicts the chosen period within the thesis. For the first sample period an average three-month Euro interbank offered rate (3M Euribor) of 0.9256% p.a. is given, whereas the second period achieves an average three-month Euribor of 0.1367% p.a..

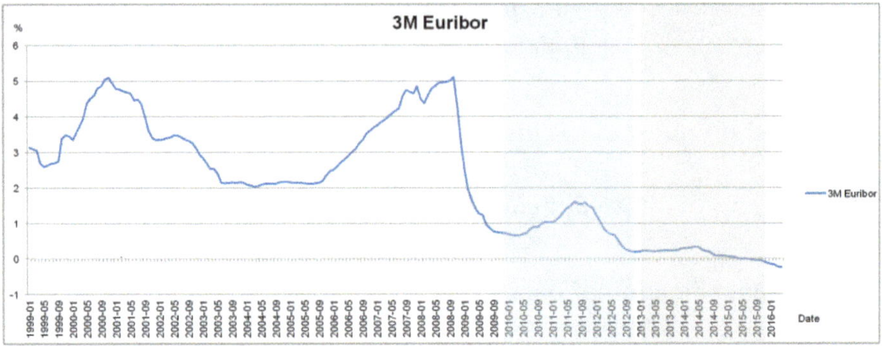


**Figure 3** Development of the three-month Euribor from 1999 to 2016

The data is analysed on a weekly basis. In the case that the data is not available on a daily frequency the last observed value carrying forward method is applied. Hence, if no data is available for a particular date the last observed value is used until new data is given. Thus the most recent observed value is used for the missing data.[52] This method has been chosen since some CDS or bond indices have missing values for a certain time point due to a lack of liquidity. However, applying the LOVCF method such particular time point are still encompassed. Thus, the available data for other CDS or bond indices can be included in the model.

The countries which are chosen to represent the European area within the analysis are Belgium, Finland, France, Ireland, Italy, Netherlands, Portugal, Spain, Sweden and United Kingdom. Thus, ten different countries will be analysed and it can be ensured that both stable and distressed economies are embedded in the analysis. Moreover, data of Germany will be used as benchmark.

52 Zhu (2006), p. 220

### 3.2.1 Data set for Hull and White model

In order to conduct the arbitrage model by Hull and White data of bonds with different maturities and the prevailing interest rate is needed.

The bond data with a maturity of one to six years is based on generic bond indices to ensure consecutive data availability. However, for certain countries and time periods no bond or data is given. Thus, the LOVCF method is applied. The countries addressed by this are Finland for a maturity of one and four years and Ireland, Italy, Portugal, Spain and Sweden for a maturity of one year. However, at the beginning of the sample period no bond data or data of a substitute bond is available for these countries. Thus, no results are calculated for these countries for a maturity of one year. In addition, no results are calculated for a maturity of four years in case of Finland.

The selected indices identified by the Bloomberg Ticker are displayed in table 2-3 within Appendix A. As benchmark for zero-default-risk rates the Treasury bond of Germany is used.

The prevailing interest rate is represented by the 3M Euribor. The Bloomberg Ticker for this instrument is given by EUR003M Index. This benchmark rate represents 2800 banks of the fifteen member states of the European Union and the Financial Markets Association.

### 3.2.2 Data set for Fontana and Scheicher model

The factor model by Fontana and Scheicher is based on six factors which are the risk-free rate, risk appetite, corporate CDS premium, debt, volatility and bid-ask spread. Moreover, CDS and bond data with maturity of five years as described within the data set needed for the Hull and White model are used in order to estimate the beta values for the factor model.

The first factor of the factor model, the risk-free rate, is represented by 3M Euribor with the Bloomberg Ticker EUR003M Index.

The risk appetite is given by the volatility index, identified by the Bloomberg Ticker VIX Index. The index is given by the Chicago Board Options Exchange and represents a market estimate of future volatility. This estimate is based on the weighted average of the implied volatilities for a wide range of strikes. As the VIX index is quoted in USD it has to be assured that the extracted data is denominated in EUR in order to be useable within the model.

The third factor, the corporate CDS premium, is represented by the iTraxx Main Investment Grade index. Therefore, the index with the Bloomberg Ticker ITRX EUR CDSI GEN 5Y Corp has been chosen for this thesis. As data for this index is available from $14^{th}$ of October 2011 onwards a substitute has to be used from $1^{st}$ of January 2010 until $14^{th}$ of October 2011 in order to cover the sample period. Therefore, the index with the Bloomberg Ticker ITRX EUR CDSI GEN 10Y Corp has been chosen. Both, the ITRX EUR CDSI GEN 5Y Corp and the ITRX EUR CDSI GEN 10Y Corp comprises 125 equally weighted CDS on investment grade European corporate entities.

The debt factor being the fourth variable within the model is represented by a country's total outstanding bonds relative to the country's gross domestic product (GDP). The available data on Bloomberg is obtained by Eurostat. As the data for this factor is only available on a monthly basis, the LOVCF method is applied in order to have the data on a weekly frequency.

Table 4 within Appendix A shows the corresponding Bloomberg Ticker for the chosen countries within the European area.

The fifth factor, the volatility, will be given by an annualised GARCH(1,1)-volatility of idiosyncratic stock returns. Therefore, the GARCH(1,1)-volatility of a certain country's stock return minus the euro area stock index will be computed. The euro area stock index is represented by the

EURO STOXX 50 Index with the Bloomberg Ticker SX5E Index. This index includes the leading blue-chip companies from twelve Eurozone countries.

Table 5 within Appendix A displays the corresponding Bloomberg Ticker for the volatility indices for each country.

The final factor within the model is given by the bid-ask spread. Therefore, the bid and ask values of the iTraxx Main Investment Grade index, represented by the Bloomberg Ticker ITRX EUR CDSI GEN 10Y Corp for the period from 1st of January 2010 until 14th of October 2011 or ITRX EUR CDSI GEN 5Y Corp from 14th of October 2011 onwards are used.

The bond data used within the Fontana and Scheicher model applied the LOVCF method for the indices of Ireland and Finland. In case of Ireland it has been used for the time period from 29th of January 2010 to 28th of January 2011. For the index of Finland the method has been applied for the time period as of 17th of May 2013 to 23th of August 2013.

As the bond data, the CDS data is based on weekly observation of generic CDS indices. The indices provide data on credit default swaps records registered in the Depository Trust and Clearing Corporation's (DTCC) Trade Information Warehouse. The chosen gross notional values indices represent the sum of CDS contracts bought or equivalently sold for all Warehouse contracts in aggregate form, by sector or for single reference entities.

Table 6 within Appendix A shows the chosen CDS indices regarding each country.

## 3.3 Implementing models

This chapter discusses how both models are implemented and which software is used. Moreover, the parameters of the models and the outcomes in case of the Hull and White model are discussed.

### 3.3.1 Hull and White

To implement the model by Hull and White for the period 2010 to 2015 the software Excel is used. Within the implementation of the model it is further assumed that no accrued interest is paid. Hence the variables $A(t)$ and $e(t)$ equal zero.

First the forward price of the $j$th bond and the present value of the loss are calculated. Subsequently, the probabilities of default for the selected countries are estimated. Therefore, the calculations are based on a recovery rate of 20.00%, 30.00% or 50.00%. Finally, the CDS spreads according to the model are obtained.

Implementing the model, it is observed that the values for the sixth year which covers the period from 1st of January 2015 to 31th of December 2015 are not reasonable. The decisive factor therefore is the negative interest rate which was prevailing in 2015. As a consequence, the sixth year is deleted as the model cannot incorporate negative interest rates. Hence, the model is calibrated for the period from 1st of January 2010 to 31th of December 2014.

The following table 1 shows the results of the spreads for the given recovery rates. No results are displayed for countries for which no data is available for the respective maturity:

**Table 1** Obtained CDS spreads in BPS applying model of Hull and White

| Belgium | | | | Finland | | | |
|---|---|---|---|---|---|---|---|
| Recovery | 20.00% | 30.00% | 50.00% | Recovery | 20.00% | 30.00% | 50.00% |
| 1 | 18.94 | 15.02 | 9.03 | 1 | - | - | - |
| 2 | 50.62 | 30.73 | 13.37 | 2 | 6.74 | 4.49 | 2.15 |
| 3 | -18.64 | -10.14 | -5.09 | 3 | -1.52 | -1.29 | -0.89 |
| 4 | -5.04 | -2.92 | -1.49 | 4 | - | - | - |
| 5 | 3.27 | 1.98 | 1.07 | 5 | 0.56 | 0.47 | 0.33 |

| France | | | |
|---|---|---|---|
| Recovery | 20.00% | 30.00% | 50.00% |
| 1 | 0.66 | 0.55 | 0.35 |
| 2 | 17.20 | 8.56 | 5.38 |
| 3 | -2.68 | -2.07 | -1.42 |
| 4 | -0.79 | -0.59 | -0.38 |
| 5 | 0.71 | 0.55 | 0.38 |

| Ireland | | | |
|---|---|---|---|
| Recovery | 20.00% | 30.00% | 50.00% |
| 1 | - | - | - |
| 2 | 16.22 | 8.92 | 3.62 |
| 3 | -11.86 | -9.06 | -5.54 |
| 4 | -25.29 | -21.30 | -13.54 |
| 5 | 1.08 | 0.87 | 0.59 |

| Italy | | | |
|---|---|---|---|
| Recovery | 20.00% | 30.00% | 50.00% |
| 1 | - | - | - |
| 2 | 58.87 | 36.37 | 16.36 |
| 3 | -10.20 | -4.79 | -2.31 |
| 4 | 10.75 | 5.25 | 2.53 |
| 5 | 16.40 | 7.67 | 3.77 |

| Netherlands | | | |
|---|---|---|---|
| T | R_20.00% | R_30.00% | R_50.00% |
| 1 | 0.53 | 0.44 | 0.28 |
| 2 | -1.56 | -1.29 | -0.77 |
| 3 | -1.07 | -0.93 | -0.66 |
| 4 | -0.07 | -0.05 | -0.02 |
| 5 | 0.33 | 0.28 | 0.20 |

| Portugal | | | |
|---|---|---|---|
| Recovery | 20.00% | 30.00% | 50.00% |
| 1 | - | - | - |
| 2 | 38.45 | 22.52 | 9.68 |
| 3 | -24.38 | -16.17 | -8.91 |
| 4 | 28.66 | 18.33 | 9.59 |
| 5 | 10.51 | 6.24 | 3.31 |

| Spain | | | |
|---|---|---|---|
| Recovery | 20.00% | 30.00% | 50.00% |
| 1 | - | - | - |
| 2 | 32.89 | 19.81 | 8.70 |
| 3 | 9.86 | 6.38 | 3.30 |
| 4 | 5.75 | 3.78 | 3.92 |
| 5 | 9.72 | 6.49 | 3.88 |

| Sweden | | | |
|---|---|---|---|
| Recovery | 20.00% | 30.00% | 50.00% |
| 1 | - | - | - |
| 2 | 11.69 | 6.73 | 2.76 |
| 3 | 4.73 | 3.75 | 2.37 |
| 4 | 5.30 | 4.23 | 2.71 |
| 5 | -2.08 | -1.70 | -1.16 |

| United Kingdom | | | |
|---|---|---|---|
| Recovery | 20.00% | 30.00% | 50.00% |
| 1 | -1.44 | -1.17 | -0.73 |
| 2 | 7.21 | 6.72 | 4.47 |
| 3 | 7.32 | 3.31 | 2.29 |
| 4 | 16.85 | 13.79 | 9.27 |
| 5 | 6.70 | 5.41 | 3.61 |

In general, the implementation of the model shows that as longer the time frame the less reliable the results are. Moreover, the calculated CDS spread is highly influenced by the risk-neutral probability of default at time $t$ which further depends on the chosen recovery rate. As the credit default swap spreads decrease by increasing the recovery rate a negative correlation is given.

In addition, based on the chosen data in some years negative CDS spreads are obtained. Calculating the differences between generic CDS indices of the selected countries and the benchmark generic CDS index negative results at some time points are given as well. In the case that the calculated CDS spreads by Hull and White are negative frequently the actual CDS spreads as difference between the generic CDS indices are also negative. Hence, the negative spreads can be ascribed to the simplification of the calculation and the model as actual CDS spreads incorporate further information.

### *3.3.2 Fontana and Scheicher*

To implement the model by Fontana and Scheicher the software R is used.

Therefore, CDS spreads are defined as the difference between the CDS index of a certain country and the benchmark CDS index given by the index of Germany. The same methodology is used to obtain the bond spreads. Thus, the bond index of a particular country minus the bond index of Germany stipulates the bond spread of that particular country.

Subsequently, a multiple linear regression for both CDS spreads and bond spreads for each selected country is conducted in order to get the beta values and the constant for the model.

The obtained values for the CDS and bond models of both sample periods are reviewed regarding their significance. Moreover, the changes of the received beta coefficients between the first and the second sample period are investigated.

The significance of the multiple linear regression as well as the results of the beta values for the selected countries for the first sample period from 2010 to 2012 are displayed within Annex B.

The analysis show that the significance for the various parameters substantially vary from country to country. However, for the CDS model the factors risk-free rate, corporate CDS premium and debt are always significant based on a significance level of at least 0.01%. The volatility parameter is significant for six countries, whereas the risk appetite is significant for four countries. The factor bid-ask spread appears to be the least frequent significant parameter within the CDS model for the first sample period.

As for the CDS model, the risk-free rate and the corporate CDS premium are the most frequent factors within the bond model regarding significance. By contrast, the risk appetite also plays a major role within the bond model compared to the CDS model. The factor bid-ask spread is also within the fixed income model the least frequent parameter concerning significance.

The plausibility of the beta values for the CDS and bond model are controlled as the values for the CDS model are quite high. However, comparing to the original model which aims to model the change of the CDSs the values seem reasonable.

The significance of the multiple linear regression as well as the results of the beta values for the selected countries for the first sample period from 2013 to 2015 are displayed within Annex C.

The most frequent significant factors within the CDS model for the second sample period are risk-free rate and corporate CDS spread followed by debt, volatility and risk appetite. Again, bid-ask spread appears to be the least frequent factor regarding significance.

A similar result is given for the bond model, however, for this period the risk appetite is besides bid-ask spread the least frequent factors as it is only significant in case of United Kingdom.

Comparing the changes of the beta values from the first to the second sample period substantial movements are given. Within the CDS models the adjustments reach form a minimum of 2.00% to 7457.00% compared to the first sample period, whereby substantial movements are frequently accompanied by a sign change of the beta value. The highest changes regarding signs are given by the model of Netherlands as all beta values reversed signs. The models of Belgium, Finland, Portugal and United Kingdom changed five to six times there signs. By contrast, the model of Sweden or Italy reversed at most once.

The most frequent high changes of beta values are given by the models of Belgium, Finland, Netherlands and Portugal. The model of France has given both the minimum and the maximum, whereby the other beta values changes by a moderate levels between 40.00% to 280.00%.The minimum change of beta values is given for the debt factor, whereas the maximum changes is given for the risk-free rate factor. Modest adjustments of beta values are given within the models of Italy and United Kingdom.

Within the bond models the adjustments vary from a minimum of 13.00% to a maximum of 3873.00%, whereby the maximum is accompanied by a sign change. The most frequent change of signs is given by the model of Sweden as all beta values reversed signs. However, the maximum changes of signs are given by three beta values excluding Sweden. The model of Ireland and Portugal reverses signs once. The most frequent high changes of beta values are given by the models of Belgium, Spain, Sweden and United Kingdom. The model of Netherlands observes the smallest adjustment for the beta value of corporate CDS premium and the highest adjustment for the beta value of debt. Moderate changes are given by the models of Finland, Ireland, Italy and Portugal.

Moreover, the linear model assumptions are tested by applying the global validation of linear models assumptions (GVLMA) package of the software R. Therefore, the global test is based on four degrees of freedom at a significance level of 0.05%. Within the validation the skewness, kurtosis, link function and the heteroscedasticity of the various models are controlled.

In the first sample period the assumption about skewness is fulfilled by the majority of the models, followed by the heteroscedasticity as six models can fulfil the criteria. The kurtosis criteria can be met by half of the models, whereas the assumption about link function is the least satisfied. The CDS models for France, Italy, Spain and Portugal satisfy the most assumptions as only one assumption cannot be fulfilled.

Within the bond models the most frequent satisfied assumption is given by kurtosis followed by skewness. The criteria about heteroscedasticity, by contrast, is the least fulfilled assumption within bond models for the first period as only four models can meet the criteria. All assumptions regarding linear model can be met by the bond model for United Kingdom.

In the second sample period the assumptions about skewness and kurtosis are commonly fulfilled by the CDS models. Subsequently, the criteria regarding heteroscedasticity followed by link function are satisfied. Within the second period three out of four assumptions can be met by the models for Ireland, Italy and Netherlands.

By contrast, within the bond models the assumption about link function is the most frequent and the assumption about skewness the least common satisfied criteria. The model for United Kingdom satisfies all assumptions regarding linear models within the second sample period.

For both periods, the most frequent fulfilled assumption is given for skewness, whereas the least satisfied criteria is given for link function within CDS models. Given the credit default swap models, Italy can satisfy the most assumptions. Within bond models, however, the models of United Kingdom can even satisfy all assumptions within both periods.

# 4 Simulation of government bond spread increase

This chapter investigates in detail the research questions. Therefore, the calibration of the model in order to examine the research questions is handled first. Subsequently, the individual impact of varying increase levels of bond yields on CDS spreads and varying interest levels is examined. Furthermore, the effect of changing both, varying increase level of bond yields including interest rates adjustments is investigated.

## 4.1 Calibration of model

In order to examine the impact of bond yields changes on the price of credit default swaps the model of Fontana and Scheicher is used. Within the model changes of the bond yields are triggered by adjustments of the risk factors. Hence, the impact of the bond yields on CDS prices is investigated by knowing these adjustments.

To obtain the results, first the increase levels of the bond yields are determined. Subsequently, the bond yields are calculated according to the model by using the obtained beta values for the respective country and sample period. The resulting yields are further adjusted by the chosen increase level. In order to obtain the changes for each risk factor causing increased bond yields, the differences between the augmented bond yields minus the original bond yields are optimised. Therefore, the sum of the differences over the sample period is minimised. The parameters which can be changed in order to optimise the sum are linked to the risk factors. Thus, each risk factor adjusted by the preserved beta value for the risk factor in question is multiplied by the corresponding parameter. The changes of the factors to their original state are hence reflected by these coefficients.

The optimisation, which is conducted in Excel, incorporates a) all parameters and b) only five parameters by excluding the risk-free rate factor in order to investigate the influence of the risk-free interest rate in particular. Moreover, the optimisation is subject to several restrictions depending on four different scenarios. Within the first scenario the changes of the risk factors reflected by the parameters are limited by 0.00% downwards and 100.00% upwards. The second scenario adds to the first one by narrowing the range of movement from 0.00% to 50.00% for the debt factor. The third scenario given by a range of -50.00% to 100.00% for the parameters includes a negative adjustment of the risk factors to the original state. The final scenario tightens the range of the previous scenario to -50.00% to 50.00%. In order to give the same starting point, the parameters are set to zero previous to the optimisation.

Having obtained the adjustments of the risk factors, one can apply the coefficients to the CDS model of the respective country and sample period. Hence the impact of an increase of the bond yields on credit risk swap prices can be examined by allocating the increase of bond yields to the risk factors.

In order to investigate the influence of varying interest rates further, the input data of the risk-free rate is adapted.

Finally, to examine the overall impact of changing increase levels and changing interest rates one combines the optimisation of the parameters and the varying input data of the risk-free rate for all four scenarios.

## 4.2 Simulation with varying increase levels

The first simulation within the thesis is concerned with the optimisation of the parameters of the risk factors. Hence, all or respectively five parameters are incorporated within the optimisation. The increase levels of the bond yields are given by 2%, 5%, 7%, 10% and 20%.

The optimisation of the parameters of the given risk factors aims to minimize the difference between the increased bond yields and the original bond yields. This is usually obtained by setting the difference to zero. However, in some scenarios the difference cannot be set to zero due to the prevailing restrictions of the parameters. Thus, similar or even equal results between scenarios for a given country are obtained. Especially the second and fourth scenario which restrict the debt factor further or respectively narrows the range of variation between -50.00% to 50.00% are concerned by this minimization issue.

The obtained parameters for the first sample period given the various restriction scenarios are displayed within Appendix D, whereas the received parameters for the second sample period are shown within Appendix E.

Given the first sample period, the difference between the increased bond yields and the original bond yields could not be set to zero for Belgium, Portugal and Sweden for the second scenario. Within the fourth scenario the changes of the CDS spreads of Portugal, Spain, Sweden and United Kingdom are concerned with the minimization issue.

Within the second sample period, the same scenarios as in the first sample period are affected by the minimization issue. Finland, Ireland, Netherlands, Portugal, Spain and United Kingdom are concerned with the issue within the second scenario. Within the fourth scenario not a single country can minimize the difference between the increased and the original CDS spread to zero.

Given the parameters, it is examined that frequently the same risk factors for the different increase levels of the bond yields are optimised within a particular country. Thus, only slight variations of the parameters are given for the various increase levels of bond yields for a given country.

Frequently high changes of the parameters for the factors of corporate CDS premium, debt and volatility are observed. Smaller adjustments of the parameters are given for the factors of risk appetite and bid-ask spread. By contrast, the parameter for the risk-free rate factor is never adjusted in order to optimise the difference between the increase bond yields and the original bond yields.

Subsequently to the optimisation of the parameters the changes of the CDS spreads are calculated. The results for the first sample period regarding changes of CDS spreads to the original state incorporating all parameters and the various scenarios are as following:

**Table 2** Results of first simulation for 2010-2012_Varying increase levels using all parameters

| 2010-2012: 1.Scenario, all parameters_change of CDS spreads to originale state | | | | | |
|---|---|---|---|---|---|
| Increase of bond yields by | 2% | 5% | 7% | 10% | 20% |
| Belgium | -155.72% | -156.73% | -157.20% | -158.20% | -161.55% |
| Finland | -94.09% | -93.97% | -93.91% | -93.79% | -93.39% |
| France | 828.58% | 845.26% | 838.85% | 855.23% | 909.82% |
| Ireland | -224.63% | -222.11% | -219.93% | -217.42% | -209.05% |
| Italy | -140.65% | -141.15% | -141.43% | -141.93% | -143.60% |
| Netherlands | -837.29% | -837.30% | -834.99% | -835.00% | -835.04% |
| Portugal | -113.25% | -114.42% | -115.07% | -116.23% | -120.09% |
| Spain | -200.11% | -200.91% | -201.39% | -202.18% | -204.83% |
| Sweden | -82.17% | -87.28% | -90.70% | -95.80% | -112.80% |
| United Kingdom | 68.01% | 66.58% | 64.57% | 63.15% | 58.42% |

| 2010-2012: 2.Scenario, all parameters_change of CDS spreads to originale state | | | | | |
|---|---|---|---|---|---|
| Increase of bond yields by | 2% | 5% | 7% | 10% | 20% |
| Belgium | -156.58% | -156.58% | -156.38% | -156.57% | -161.55% |
| Finland | -94.09% | -93.97% | -93.91% | -93.79% | -93.39% |
| France | 828.58% | 845.26% | 838.85% | 855.23% | 909.82% |
| Ireland | -224.63% | -222.11% | -219.93% | -217.42% | -214.15% |
| Italy | -140.65% | -141.15% | -141.43% | -141.93% | -143.60% |
| Netherlands | -837.29% | -837.30% | -834.99% | -835.00% | -835.04% |
| Portugal | -411.60% | -411.60% | -408.99% | -408.99% | -408.99% |
| Spain | -200.11% | -200.91% | -201.39% | -202.18% | -204.83% |
| Sweden | 168.25% | 168.25% | 167.73% | 167.73% | 167.73% |
| United Kingdom | 122.44% | 122.46% | 121.05% | 121.07% | 121.14% |

| 2010-2012: 3.Scenario, all parameters_change of CDS spreads to originale state | | | | | |
|---|---|---|---|---|---|
| Increase of bond yields by | 2% | 5% | 7% | 10% | 20% |
| Belgium | -164.11% | -164.98% | -165.33% | -166.20% | -169.10% |
| Finland | -90.49% | -90.48% | -90.51% | -90.50% | -90.46% |
| France | 1154.92% | 1166.39% | 1150.68% | 1161.95% | 1199.50% |
| Ireland | -251.56% | -249.86% | -248.10% | -246.41% | -240.76% |
| Italy | -149.20% | -149.59% | -149.79% | -150.18% | -151.48% |
| Netherlands | -864.89% | -865.20% | -863.00% | -863.30% | -864.33% |
| Portugal | -115.76% | -117.09% | -117.83% | -119.15% | -123.54% |
| Spain | -202.34% | -203.18% | -203.69% | -204.53% | -207.34% |
| Sweden | -30.87% | -27.66% | -25.66% | -22.45% | -11.76% |
| United Kingdom | 68.01% | 66.58% | 64.57% | 63.15% | 58.42% |

| 2010-2012: 4.Scenario, all parameters_change of CDS spreads to originale state | | | | | |
|---|---|---|---|---|---|
| Increase of bond yields by | 2% | 5% | 7% | 10% | 20% |
| Belgium | -164.11% | -164.98% | -165.33% | -166.20% | -169.10% |
| Finland | -90.49% | -90.48% | -90.51% | -90.50% | -90.46% |
| France | 1154.92% | 1166.39% | 1150.68% | 1161.95% | 1199.50% |
| Ireland | -251.56% | -249.86% | -248.10% | -246.41% | -240.76% |
| Italy | -149.20% | -149.59% | -149.79% | -150.18% | -151.48% |
| Netherlands | -864.89% | -865.20% | -863.00% | -863.30% | -864.33% |
| Portugal | -409.22% | -409.22% | -406.63% | -406.63% | -406.63% |
| Spain | -243.70% | -243.70% | -243.63% | -243.63% | -243.63% |
| Sweden | 149.44% | 149.44% | 148.95% | 148.95% | 148.95% |
| United Kingdom | 121.24% | 121.24% | 119.83% | 119.83% | 119.83% |

Given the results of the CDS changes, it can be examined that the increase of bond yields is negatively correlated to the CDS spreads. Exceptions thereof are France and United Kingdom within all scenarios and Sweden within the second and fourth scenario.

A modest change of CDS spreads is given for Finland, Sweden and United Kingdom within all scenarios. By contrast, a substantial adaption of the CDS spreads is observed for France and Netherlands within all scenarios and Portugal within the second and fourth scenario.

Based on the results it can be stated that a percentage change of bond yields results in a substantial movement of the CDS spreads for a particular country compared to the bond yield increase. However, the changes of the CDS spreads between the various increase levels increase on a considerably smaller scale than the given increase levels of bond yields. In the case of Finland even a decrease of CDS spread changes for a higher increase of bond yields is given. A steady decrease of CDS spread changes is observed for Ireland. Sweden also examines declining CDS spread changes within the second and third scenario. The same movement is observed for United Kingdom, excluding the second scenario.

The optimisation of five parameters results to following changes of CDS spreads for the various scenarios:

**Table 3** Results of first simulation for 2010-2012_Varying increase levels using five parameters

| 2010-2012: 1.Scenario, five parameters_change of CDS spreads to originale state | | | | | |
|---|---|---|---|---|---|
| Increase of bond yields by | 2% | 5% | 7% | 10% | 20% |
| Belgium | -154.90% | -155.89% | -156.56% | -157.56% | -158.53% |
| Finland | -93.81% | -93.69% | -93.61% | -93.49% | -97.83% |
| France | 765.93% | 781.47% | 791.83% | 807.37% | 755.99% |
| Ireland | -222.37% | -219.88% | -218.22% | -215.72% | -150.90% |
| Italy | -139.98% | -140.48% | -140.81% | -141.30% | -140.50% |
| Netherlands | -816.88% | -817.18% | -817.39% | -817.69% | -496.13% |
| Portugal | -112.49% | -113.64% | -114.40% | -115.54% | -119.61% |
| Spain | -196.67% | -197.54% | -198.12% | -198.98% | -151.85% |
| Sweden | -83.36% | -88.42% | -91.79% | -96.86% | -113.73% |
| United Kingdom | 74.09% | 72.68% | 71.73% | 70.32% | -70.12% |

| 2010-2012: 2.Scenario, five parameters_change of CDS spreads to originale state | | | | | |
|---|---|---|---|---|---|
| Increase of bond yields by | 2% | 5% | 7% | 10% | 20% |
| Belgium | -156.26% | -156.26% | -156.26% | -156.26% | -158.53% |
| Finland | -93.81% | -93.69% | -93.61% | -93.49% | -97.83% |
| France | 765.93% | 781.47% | 791.83% | 807.37% | 755.99% |
| Ireland | -222.37% | -219.88% | -218.22% | -215.72% | -213.47% |
| Italy | -139.98% | -140.48% | -140.81% | -141.30% | -140.50% |
| Netherlands | -816.88% | -817.18% | -817.39% | -817.69% | -496.13% |
| Portugal | -406.05% | -406.05% | -406.05% | -406.05% | -406.05% |
| Spain | -196.67% | -197.54% | -198.12% | -198.98% | -151.85% |
| Sweden | 165.78% | 165.78% | 165.78% | 165.78% | 165.78% |
| United Kingdom | 119.54% | 119.56% | 119.57% | 119.59% | 119.79% |

| 2010-2012: 3.Scenario, five parameters_change of CDS spreads to originale state | | | | | |
|---|---|---|---|---|---|
| Increase of bond yields by | 2% | 5% | 7% | 10% | 20% |
| Belgium | -163.66% | -164.53% | -165.11% | -165.97% | -168.86% |
| Finland | -90.63% | -90.62% | -90.62% | -90.61% | -90.57% |
| France | 1069.41% | 1080.10% | 1087.22% | 1097.91% | 1133.54% |
| Ireland | -250.37% | -248.68% | -247.56% | -245.88% | -240.26% |
| Italy | -149.07% | -149.46% | -149.72% | -150.12% | -151.42% |
| Netherlands | -858.54% | -858.84% | -859.05% | -859.35% | -860.37% |
| Portugal | -115.42% | -116.72% | -117.59% | -118.89% | -123.24% |
| Spain | -201.94% | -202.78% | -203.34% | -204.17% | -206.96% |
| Sweden | -31.49% | -28.31% | -26.18% | -22.99% | -12.37% |
| United Kingdom | 65.57% | 64.16% | 63.22% | 61.80% | 57.09% |

| 2010-2012: 4.Scenario, five parameters_change of CDS spreads to originale state | | | | | |
|---|---|---|---|---|---|
| Increase of bond yields by | 2% | 5% | 7% | 10% | 20% |
| Belgium | -163.66% | -164.53% | -165.11% | -165.97% | -168.86% |
| Finland | -90.63% | -90.62% | -90.62% | -90.61% | -90.57% |
| France | 1069.41% | 1080.10% | 1087.22% | 1097.91% | 1133.54% |
| Ireland | -250.37% | -248.68% | -247.56% | -245.88% | -240.26% |
| Italy | -149.07% | -149.46% | -149.72% | -150.12% | -151.42% |
| Netherlands | -858.54% | -858.84% | -859.05% | -859.35% | -860.37% |
| Portugal | -403.74% | -403.74% | -403.74% | -403.74% | -403.74% |
| Spain | -243.14% | -243.14% | -243.14% | -243.14% | -243.14% |
| Sweden | 147.15% | 147.15% | 147.15% | 147.15% | 147.15% |
| United Kingdom | 118.75% | 118.75% | 118.75% | 118.75% | 118.75% |

The optimisation incorporating five parameters caused very similar results as received by incorporating all parameters due to the fact that the parameter for the risk-free factor has not been modified by the optimisation involving all parameters. A reason therefore may be the small portion for which the risk-free rate factor accounts within the models.

A negative correlation between bond yields and CDS spreads can be observed, excluding France and United Kingdom within all scenarios and Sweden within the second and fourth scenario.

The lowest CDS spread changes are observed by Finland, Sweden and United Kingdom, whereas France examines the highest CDS spread modifications followed by Netherlands. The variation of the CDS spread changes along with the increasing level of bond yields declines for Ireland and United Kingdom. Netherlands examines a substantial decrease of CDS spread change within the bond yield increase of 10% to 20% for the first scenario.

Comparing the optimisation incorporating all parameters against involving five parameters a slight decrease of CDS spread changes is given. For higher CDS spread changes the decline expands as it can be observed by France. Exceptions thereof are the changes of CDS spreads for Sweden and United Kingdom in the first scenario and Sweden for the third scenario. Thus, including the risk-free rate results frequently in a modest increase of CDS spread changes even though the increase level has been kept stable.

For the second sample period, following result of CDS spread changes are obtained involving all parameters in the optimisation process:

**Table 4** Results of first simulation for 2013-2015_Varying increase levels using all parameters

| 2013-2015: 1.Scenario, all parameters_change of CDS spreads to originale state | | | | | |
|---|---|---|---|---|---|
| Increase of bond yields by | 2% | 5% | 7% | 10% | 20% |
| Belgium | -103.37% | -103.21% | -103.11% | -102.95% | -102.44% |
| Finland | -95.62% | -96.22% | -95.68% | -96.43% | -98.95% |
| France | 222.76% | 219.39% | 205.52% | 202.28% | 191.47% |
| Ireland | -107.92% | -107.56% | -107.38% | -107.02% | -105.81% |
| Italy | -254.80% | -253.53% | -252.32% | -251.05% | -246.83% |
| Netherlands | -120.46% | -120.41% | -120.27% | -120.21% | -120.04% |
| Portugal | -92.39% | -91.03% | -90.06% | -88.68% | -84.10% |
| Spain | -104.65% | -104.46% | -103.96% | -103.79% | -103.22% |
| Sweden | -100.47% | -100.70% | -100.85% | -101.08% | -101.85% |
| United Kingdom | -114.00% | -114.17% | -114.17% | -114.34% | -114.89% |
| 2013-2015: 2.Scenario, all parameters_change of CDS spreads to originale state | | | | | |
| Increase of bond yields by | 2% | 5% | 7% | 10% | 20% |
| Belgium | -105.03% | -104.90% | -104.82% | -104.69% | -104.27% |
| Finland | -37.64% | -37.64% | -20.41% | -20.41% | -20.41% |
| France | 336.01% | 336.13% | 320.21% | 320.33% | 320.72% |
| Ireland | -162.07% | -162.07% | -162.54% | -162.54% | -162.54% |
| Italy | -254.80% | -253.53% | -252.32% | -251.05% | -246.83% |
| Netherlands | -82.96% | -82.96% | -83.05% | -83.05% | -83.05% |
| Portugal | -69.76% | -69.76% | -69.57% | -69.57% | -69.57% |
| Spain | -150.38% | -150.38% | -145.94% | -145.94% | -145.94% |
| Sweden | -74.18% | -73.95% | -73.96% | -73.73% | -72.97% |
| United Kingdom | -71.25% | -71.25% | -71.48% | -71.48% | -71.48% |

| 2013-2015: 3.Scenario, all parameters_change of CDS spreads to originale state | | | | | |
|---|---|---|---|---|---|
| Increase of bond yields by | 2% | 5% | 7% | 10% | 20% |
| Belgium | -102.39% | -102.23% | -102.12% | -101.96% | -101.43% |
| Finland | -85.41% | -85.31% | -81.16% | -81.03% | -80.60% |
| France | 223.92% | 220.56% | 206.65% | 203.41% | 192.63% |
| Ireland | -107.94% | -107.59% | -107.40% | -107.04% | -105.84% |
| Italy | -255.56% | -254.31% | -253.10% | -251.85% | -247.67% |
| Netherlands | -120.46% | -120.41% | -120.27% | -120.21% | -120.04% |
| Portugal | -91.34% | -90.01% | -89.01% | -87.62% | -82.96% |
| Spain | -104.71% | -104.53% | -104.02% | -103.85% | -103.29% |
| Sweden | -99.85% | -100.08% | -100.23% | -100.46% | -101.21% |
| United Kingdom | -115.21% | -115.38% | -115.38% | -115.55% | -116.11% |

| 2013-2015: 4.Scenario, all parameters_change of CDS spreads to originale state | | | | | |
|---|---|---|---|---|---|
| Increase of bond yields by | 2% | 5% | 7% | 10% | 20% |
| Belgium | -93.29% | -93.29% | -93.29% | -93.29% | -93.29% |
| Finland | -44.20% | -44.20% | -28.78% | -28.78% | -28.78% |
| France | 348.39% | 348.39% | 331.95% | 331.95% | 331.95% |
| Ireland | -175.46% | -175.46% | -176.03% | -176.03% | -176.03% |
| Italy | -215.56% | -215.56% | -215.28% | -215.28% | -215.28% |
| Netherlands | -96.39% | -96.39% | -96.41% | -96.41% | -96.41% |
| Portugal | -96.74% | -96.74% | -96.72% | -96.72% | -96.72% |
| Spain | -155.09% | -155.09% | -150.24% | -150.24% | -150.24% |
| Sweden | -78.94% | -78.94% | -79.07% | -79.07% | -79.07% |
| United Kingdom | -80.68% | -80.68% | -80.83% | -80.83% | -80.83% |

Within all scenarios, a negative correlation between the increase of bond yields and the CDS spreads is examined with the sole exception of France.

A modest change of CDS spreads is given for Finland and Portugal for all scenarios. Netherlands, Sweden and United Kingdom examine a moderate change of CDS spreads in the second, fourth and respectively in the third scenario in case of Sweden. By contrast, a substantial adaption of the CDS spreads is observed for France and Italy within all scenarios.

Given the results, it can be examined that the bond yield changes results in substantial movements of the CDS spreads for a particular country. However, compared to the first sample period the changes of CDS spreads are on a substantially smaller scale. The CDS spread changes frequently decline by increasing bond yields within the second sample period. Exemptions thereof are Finland, Ireland, Netherlands, Sweden and United Kingdom, whereas only United Kingdom increased CDS spreads with bond yields for all scenarios.

The optimisation of five parameters results in following changes of CDS spreads for the various scenarios:

**Table 5** Results of first simulation for 2013-2015_Varying increase levels using five parameters

| 2013-2015: 1.Scenario, five parameters_change of CDS spreads to originale state | | | | | |
|---|---|---|---|---|---|
| Increase of bond yields by | 2% | 5% | 7% | 10% | 20% |
| Belgium | -104.42% | -104.27% | -104.16% | -104.01% | -100.56% |
| Finland | -95.90% | -96.49% | -96.02% | -96.78% | -99.30% |
| France | 246.15% | 242.79% | 228.06% | 224.82% | -31.80% |
| Ireland | -109.01% | -108.65% | -108.48% | -108.12% | -106.29% |
| Italy | -249.69% | -248.42% | -247.22% | -245.96% | -145.89% |
| Netherlands | -121.28% | -121.22% | -121.08% | -121.03% | -120.15% |
| Portugal | -94.09% | -92.72% | -91.75% | -90.37% | -84.90% |
| Spain | -105.11% | -104.59% | -104.07% | -103.90% | -103.19% |
| Sweden | -99.44% | -99.67% | -99.82% | -100.05% | -111.31% |
| United Kingdom | -113.78% | -113.95% | -113.95% | -114.12% | -114.87% |

| 2013-2015: 2.Scenario, five parameters_change of CDS spreads to originale state | | | | | |
|---|---|---|---|---|---|
| Increase of bond yields by | 2% | 5% | 7% | 10% | 20% |
| Belgium | -105.87% | -105.75% | -105.66% | -105.54% | -104.37% |
| Finland | -37.58% | -37.58% | -20.33% | -20.33% | -20.33% |
| France | 336.04% | 336.16% | 320.24% | 320.36% | 321.47% |
| Ireland | -162.14% | -162.14% | -162.61% | -162.61% | -162.61% |
| Italy | -249.69% | -248.42% | -247.22% | -245.96% | -217.31% |
| Netherlands | -82.97% | -82.97% | -83.06% | -83.06% | -83.06% |
| Portugal | -69.71% | -69.71% | -69.53% | -69.53% | -69.53% |
| Spain | -150.32% | -150.32% | -145.89% | -145.89% | -145.89% |
| Sweden | -75.30% | -75.07% | -75.07% | -74.84% | -73.35% |
| United Kingdom | -71.29% | -71.29% | -71.52% | -71.52% | -71.52% |

| 2013-2015: 3.Scenario, five parameters_change of CDS spreads to originale state | | | | | |
|---|---|---|---|---|---|
| Increase of bond yields by | 2% | 5% | 7% | 10% | 20% |
| Belgium | -102.29% | -102.13% | -102.03% | -101.87% | -101.33% |
| Finland | -85.33% | -85.23% | -81.06% | -80.93% | -80.50% |
| France | 224.33% | 220.97% | 207.05% | 203.81% | 193.03% |
| Ireland | -107.99% | -107.63% | -107.45% | -107.09% | -105.88% |
| Italy | -255.58% | -254.33% | -253.12% | -251.87% | -247.69% |
| Netherlands | -120.48% | -120.42% | -120.28% | -120.23% | -120.05% |
| Portugal | -91.33% | -90.04% | -89.05% | -87.65% | -83.00% |
| Spain | -104.65% | -104.47% | -103.96% | -103.80% | -103.24% |
| Sweden | -99.85% | -100.07% | -100.23% | -100.45% | -101.21% |
| United Kingdom | -115.25% | -115.42% | -115.41% | -115.58% | -116.14% |

| 2013-2015: 4.Scenario, five parameters_change of CDS spreads to originale state | | | | | |
|---|---|---|---|---|---|
| Increase of bond yields by | 2% | 5% | 7% | 10% | 20% |
| Belgium | -93.18% | -93.18% | -93.18% | -93.18% | -93.18% |
| Finland | -44.14% | -44.14% | -28.70% | -28.70% | -28.70% |
| France | 348.61% | 348.61% | 332.16% | 332.16% | 332.16% |
| Ireland | -175.52% | -175.52% | -176.10% | -176.10% | -176.10% |
| Italy | -215.56% | -215.56% | -215.28% | -215.28% | -215.28% |
| Netherlands | -96.40% | -96.40% | -96.42% | -96.42% | -96.42% |
| Portugal | -96.70% | -96.70% | -96.68% | -96.68% | -96.68% |
| Spain | -155.03% | -155.03% | -150.18% | -150.18% | -150.18% |
| Sweden | -78.96% | -78.96% | -79.09% | -79.09% | -79.09% |
| United Kingdom | -80.71% | -80.71% | -80.87% | -80.87% | -80.87% |

Excluding France, a negative relation between the increase of bond yields and CDS spreads is prevailing.

Modest CDS spread changes are observed by Finland, Portugal, Netherlands Sweden and United Kingdom within varying scenarios. Higher adjustments of CDS spreads are observed for France and Italy. The CDS spread changes frequently decline by increasing the bond yields within the second sample period. Exemptions thereof are Finland, Ireland, Sweden and United Kingdom. Yet, only United Kingdom increase CDS spreads along with bond yields for all scenarios and Sweden within three scenarios.

Comparing the CDS spread changes involving five parameters to the previous analyses of using all parameters an indifferent development is observed. Thus, within the first and second scenario the majority of the countries increase their CDS spread changes. Within the last two scenarios countries which increase and decrease their CDS spread changes are balanced. France, Ireland and Netherlands are kept stable by increasing CDS spread changes over all scenarios.

Comparing the sample periods, it can be examined that the CDS spread changes decrease to a more modest level within the second period.

## 4.3 Simulation with varying interest levels

The second simulation, which incorporates all parameters, focuses on the effect of varying interest levels on the CDS spreads. Therefore, a parallel shift and a twist of the prevailing interest rate curves for the given sample periods are performed. In the first case, the interest rate curves is shifted upwards by 0.20%, 0.50%, 0.70%, 1.00% and 2.00%. In the second case, the interest rate curve is increased by 2.00%, 5.00%, 7.00%, 10.00% and 20.00% which resulted in a strengthening of the prevailing twist. The variations of the interest rate curves are displayed in the following graphs:

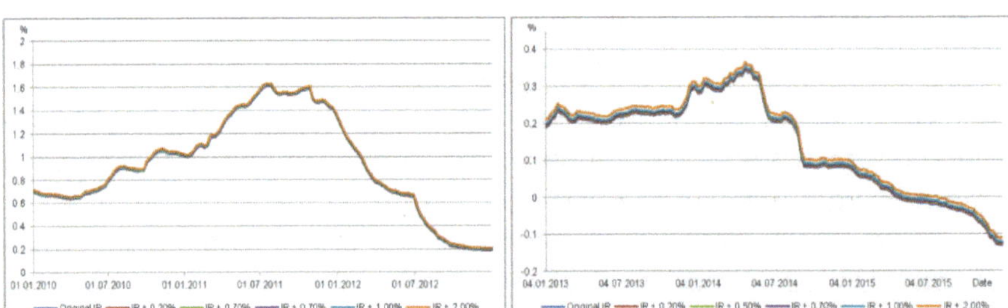


**Figure 4** Parallel shift of interest rate curves for both sample periods

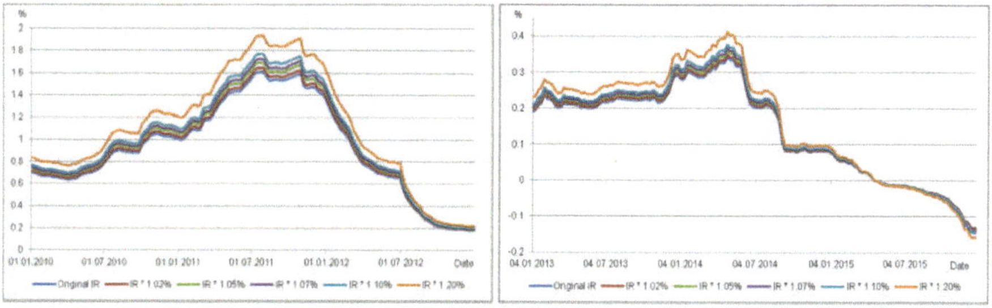

**Figure 5** Twist of interest rate curves for both sample periods

Given the graphs, it is obvious that within the first sample period the parallel shift only shows small movements which marginally enhance in the second sample period. By contrast, an increase of the prevailing interest rate curves by a certain percentage point results in an enhancement of high interest rates, whereas low interest rates hardly change. A twist of the curve is given by an interest rate around zero.

Following results are obtained in case of a parallel shift or respectively for a twist of the interest rate curve for the first sample period:

**Table 6** Results of second simulation for 2010-2012_Parallel shift of interest rate

| 2010-2012: Parallel shift_change of CDS spreads to originale state | | | | | |
|---|---|---|---|---|---|
| Parallel shift of interest rate | 0.20% | 0.50% | 0.70% | 1.00% | 2.00% |
| Belgium | -218.76% | -218.83% | -218.46% | -218.53% | -218.78% |
| Finland | -90.15% | -90.18% | -90.23% | -90.26% | -90.36% |
| France | 1874.01% | 1873.99% | 1837.78% | 1837.76% | 1837.70% |
| Ireland | -307.55% | -307.61% | -306.77% | -306.83% | -307.02% |
| Italy | -180.25% | -180.26% | -180.17% | -180.18% | -180.22% |
| Netherlands | -836.15% | -836.13% | -833.80% | -833.78% | -833.70% |
| Portugal | -658.89% | -658.96% | -654.32% | -654.39% | -654.61% |
| Spain | -162.41% | -162.29% | -162.18% | -162.06% | -161.65% |
| Sweden | 363.06% | 362.92% | 361.92% | 361.77% | 361.29% |
| United Kingdom | 342.34% | 342.27% | 339.40% | 339.33% | 339.10% |

**Table 7** Results of second simulation for 2010-2012_Twist of interest rate

| 2010-2012: Twist_change of CDS spreads to originale state | | | | | |
|---|---|---|---|---|---|
| Twist of interest rate by | 2.00% | 5.00% | 7.00% | 10.00% | 20.00% |
| Belgium | -219.17% | -219.85% | -219.88% | -220.57% | -222.85% |
| Finland | -90.32% | -90.60% | -90.82% | -91.11% | -92.05% |
| France | 1873.90% | 1873.72% | 1837.41% | 1837.23% | 1836.63% |
| Ireland | -307.87% | -308.39% | -307.86% | -308.38% | -310.12% |
| Italy | -180.31% | -180.42% | -180.39% | -180.49% | -180.84% |
| Netherlands | -836.03% | -835.82% | -833.37% | -833.16% | -832.47% |
| Portugal | -659.27% | -659.89% | -655.61% | -656.23% | -658.29% |
| Spain | -161.74% | -160.62% | -159.85% | -158.73% | -155.00% |
| Sweden | 362.26% | 360.91% | 359.11% | 357.77% | 353.28% |
| United Kingdom | 341.96% | 341.31% | 338.07% | 337.43% | 335.31% |

Given the changes of CDS spreads for the first period a negative correlation between bond yields and CDS spreads for both a parallel shift or respectively twist of the interest rate curve is frequently given. Exemptions thereof are France, Sweden and United Kingdom.

Modest changes of spreads are observed for Finland, whereas France, Netherlands and Portugal substantially adapt their CDS premiums. In particular France is very sensitive to changes of bond yields. However, CDS spread changes do not substantially increase by augmenting the increase level of bond yields. Indeed, in case of a parallel shift only CDS spread changes of Belgium and Finland slightly increased. Italy, Portugal and Spain observed a decrease of CDS spread changes followed by an increase for the highest increase levels of bond yields. France, Ireland, Netherland, Sweden and United Kingdom even experience a slight decrease of credit default swap spread changes.

In case of a twist of the interest rate curve Belgium, Finland, Ireland and Italy examine an increase of CDS spread changes along with rising bond yields. CDS spread changes of Portugal are very indifferent, whereas France, Netherlands, Spain, Sweden and United Kingdom encountered a decrease of changes.

Comparing both modifications of interest rate curves it can be stated that a twist results in a smaller overall change of CDS spreads for Netherlands, Spain, Sweden and United Kingdom. By contrast, Belgium,

Finland, France, Ireland, Italy, Portugal observe an increase of changes. Hence, a twist of the interest rate curve results in rising CDS spreads for the majority of countries.

For the second sample period following results are obtained in case of a parallel shift or respectively for a twist of the interest rate curve:

**Table 8** Results of second simulation for 2013-2015_Parallel shift of interest rate

| 2013-2015: Parallel shift_change of CDS spreads to originale state | | | | | |
|---|---|---|---|---|---|
| Parallel shift of interest rate | 0.20% | 0.50% | 0.70% | 1.00% | 2.00% |
| Belgium | -133.63% | -133.38% | -133.21% | -132.95% | -132.10% |
| Finland | -16.88% | -16.73% | 6.41% | 6.60% | 7.24% |
| France | 791.02% | 791.55% | 759.20% | 759.71% | 761.42% |
| Ireland | -263.07% | -263.24% | -264.59% | -264.76% | -265.32% |
| Italy | -324.77% | -324.70% | -324.24% | -324.24% | -324.26% |
| Netherlands | -92.81% | -92.83% | -92.88% | -92.90% | -92.97% |
| Portugal | -148.88% | -148.78% | -149.01% | -148.90% | -148.56% |
| Spain | -203.90% | -203.75% | -194.53% | -194.40% | -193.95% |
| Sweden | -68.04% | -68.09% | -68.32% | -68.37% | -68.53% |
| United Kingdom | -17.76% | -17.84% | -18.55% | -18.63% | -18.90% |

**Table 9** Results of second simulation for 2013-2015_Twist of interest rate

| 2013-2015: Twist_change of CDS spreads to originale state | | | | | |
|---|---|---|---|---|---|
| Twist of interest rate by | 2.00% | 5.00% | 7.00% | 10.00% | 20.00% |
| Belgium | -133.57% | -133.22% | -132.99% | -132.64% | -131.48% |
| Finland | -16.84% | -16.64% | 6.58% | 6.84% | 7.71% |
| France | 791.15% | 791.88% | 759.64% | 760.34% | 762.67% |
| Ireland | -263.11% | -263.34% | -264.73% | -264.96% | -265.74% |
| Italy | -324.77% | -324.78% | -324.24% | -324.25% | -324.27% |
| Netherlands | -92.81% | -92.84% | -92.90% | -92.93% | -93.02% |
| Portugal | -148.85% | -148.71% | -148.92% | -148.78% | -148.31% |
| Spain | -203.86% | -203.66% | -194.42% | -194.23% | -193.62% |
| Sweden | -68.06% | -68.12% | -68.36% | -68.43% | -68.65% |
| United Kingdom | -17.78% | -17.89% | -18.62% | -18.73% | -19.10% |

A negative correlation between bond yields and CDS spreads for both modifications of the interest rate curve excluding France is observed.

Modest changes of spreads are given for Finland, Netherlands, Sweden and United Kingdom. By contrast, a substantially adaption of CDS spread changes is given for France. Given the various increase levels of the interest rate curve the CDS spread changes hardly alter. However, an upward movement of CDS spread changes along with bond yields for both parallel shift and twist of the interest rate curve is given for Ireland, Netherlands, Sweden and United Kingdom. An indifferent adjustment of CDS changes is observed for Finland, France, Italy and Portugal. In case of Belgium and Spain the changes even decrease with increasing levels of the interest rate curve.

Comparing both modifications of the interest rate curve a twist causes a decrease of CDS spread changes for Finland, Portugal and Spain. Higher CDS spreads are observed for Belgium, France, Ireland, Sweden and United Kingdom. In addition, Italy and Netherlands experience increasing CDS spreads at a modification of interest rates of 10% or respectively 5%.

Given the first and the second sample period it can be stated that for both periods a twist of the interest rate results in rising CDS spreads for the majority of countries.

## 4.4 Simulation with varying interest levels and varying increase levels

The third simulation incorporates all parameters of the risk factors from the first simulation and the modification of the interest rate curve from the second simulation. Thus, the minimization issue prevailing within the first simulation is valid for the third simulation given the second and fourth scenario as well.

Within the first sample period, the minimization issue concerns the results of Belgium, Portugal, Spain, Sweden and United Kingdom. Finland, Ireland, Netherlands, Portugal, Spain and United Kingdom or even all countries within the fourth scenario are affected in the second sample period.

Following results for the first sample period incorporating the optimisation of parameters and the shift of the interest rate curve are obtained:

**Table 10** Results of third simulation for 2010-2012_Optimisation and parallel shift of interest rate

| 2010-2012: 1.Scenario, Shift_change of CDS spreads to originale state | | | | | |
|---|---|---|---|---|---|
| Increase of bond yields by | 2% | 5% | 7% | 10% | 20% |
| Parallel shift of interest rate | 0.20% | 0.50% | 0.70% | 1.00% | 2.00% |
| Belgium | -155.77% | -156.85% | -157.37% | -158.45% | -162.04% |
| Finland | -94.11% | -94.02% | -93.98% | -93.89% | -93.59% |
| France | 828.56% | 845.23% | 838.80% | 855.16% | 909.69% |
| Ireland | -224.67% | -222.21% | -220.06% | -217.60% | -209.43% |
| Italy | -140.66% | -141.17% | -141.46% | -141.97% | -143.67% |
| Netherlands | -837.27% | -837.26% | -834.94% | -834.93% | -834.89% |
| Portugal | -113.30% | -114.53% | -115.23% | -116.45% | -120.53% |
| Spain | -200.03% | -200.71% | -201.11% | -201.78% | -204.03% |
| Sweden | -82.26% | -87.52% | -91.04% | -96.28% | -113.77% |
| United Kingdom | 67.97% | 66.47% | 64.41% | 62.92% | 57.96% |

| 2010-2012: 2.Scenario, Shift_change of CDS spreads to originale state | | | | | |
|---|---|---|---|---|---|
| Increase of bond yields by | 2.00% | 5.00% | 7.00% | 10.00% | 20.00% |
| Parallel shift of interest rate | 0.20% | 0.50% | 0.70% | 1.00% | 2.00% |
| Belgium | -156.63% | -156.71% | -156.55% | -156.81% | -162.04% |
| Finland | -94.11% | -94.02% | -93.98% | -93.89% | -93.59% |
| France | 828.56% | 845.23% | 838.80% | 855.16% | 909.69% |
| Ireland | -224.67% | -222.21% | -220.06% | -217.60% | -214.53% |
| Italy | -140.66% | -141.17% | -141.46% | -141.97% | -143.67% |
| Netherlands | -837.27% | -837.26% | -834.94% | -834.93% | -834.89% |
| Portugal | -411.64% | -411.71% | -409.14% | -409.21% | -409.43% |
| Spain | -200.03% | -200.71% | -201.11% | -201.78% | -204.03% |
| Sweden | 168.15% | 168.01% | 167.39% | 167.24% | 166.76% |
| United Kingdom | 122.39% | 122.34% | 120.89% | 120.84% | 120.68% |

| 2010-2012: 3.Scenario, Shift_change of CDS spreads to originale state | | | | | |
|---|---|---|---|---|---|
| Increase of bond yields by | 2% | 5% | 7% | 10% | 20% |
| Parallel shift of interest rate | 0.20% | 0.50% | 0.70% | 1.00% | 2.00% |
| Belgium | -164.16% | -165.10% | -165.50% | -166.44% | -169.59% |
| Finland | -90.51% | -90.53% | -90.58% | -90.60% | -90.66% |
| France | 1154.90% | 1166.36% | 1150.64% | 1161.88% | 1199.37% |
| Ireland | -251.60% | -249.96% | -248.23% | -246.59% | -241.14% |
| Italy | -149.20% | -149.61% | -149.81% | -150.21% | -151.56% |
| Netherlands | -864.87% | -865.16% | -862.94% | -863.23% | -864.18% |
| Portugal | -115.81% | -117.20% | -117.98% | -119.37% | -123.98% |
| Spain | -202.26% | -202.98% | -203.41% | -204.13% | -206.53% |
| Sweden | -30.97% | -27.90% | -26.00% | -22.93% | -12.72% |
| United Kingdom | 67.97% | 66.47% | 64.41% | 62.92% | 57.96% |

| 2010-2012: 4.Scenario, Shift_change of CDS spreads to originale state | | | | | |
|---|---|---|---|---|---|
| Increase of bond yields by | 2% | 5% | 7% | 10% | 20% |
| Parallel shift of interest rate | 0.20% | 0.50% | 0.70% | 1.00% | 2.00% |
| Belgium | -164.16% | -165.10% | -165.50% | -166.44% | -169.59% |
| Finland | -90.51% | -90.53% | -90.58% | -90.60% | -90.66% |
| France | 1154.90% | 1166.36% | 1150.64% | 1161.88% | 1199.37% |
| Ireland | -251.60% | -249.96% | -248.23% | -246.59% | -241.14% |
| Italy | -149.20% | -149.61% | -149.81% | -150.21% | -151.56% |
| Netherlands | -864.87% | -865.16% | -862.94% | -863.23% | -864.18% |
| Portugal | -409.26% | -409.33% | -406.78% | -406.85% | -407.07% |
| Spain | -243.62% | -243.50% | -243.35% | -243.23% | -242.83% |
| Sweden | 149.35% | 149.20% | 148.62% | 148.47% | 147.99% |
| United Kingdom | 121.20% | 121.13% | 119.67% | 119.60% | 119.37% |

Incorporating the optimised parameters and the parallel shift of the interest rate curve a negative correlation between bond yields and CDS spreads is still experienced. Exceptions thereof are excluding France and United Kingdom in all scenarios and Sweden within the second and fourth scenario.

Moreover, modest CDS spread changes are still prevailing for Finland, Sweden and United Kingdom, whereas France and Netherlands examine high modifications.

However, the development of the CDS spread along with the increase of bond yields and parallel shift of interest rate causes a different result as given within the first simulation for the third and fourth scenario. Thus, the movements of CDS spreads along with bond yields are quite unstable or even reverse for Finland, Netherlands, Portugal and Spain. Especially for

Finland it can be observed that the development of the CDS spreads corresponds to the parallel shift of interest rates.

Comparing the levels of CDS spread changes to the first simulation, the CDS spread changes mainly increase excluding Netherlands and Spain. By contrast, comparing the levels of CDS spread changes to the second simulation Belgium, Finland and Netherlands observe higher CDS spread changes in all scenarios. Spain examines an increase of CDS spreads with higher increase levels. Portugal exhibits higher CDS spread changes in the second and fourth scenario, whereas Sweden experiences an increase of CDS spreads in the first scenario. However, the majority of the countries experienced a decrease of CDS spread changes. Thus, comparing the first and the third simulation frequently higher CDS spread changes are given, whereas the comparison of the second and third simulation results in a decrease of changes.

Incorporating the optimisation of parameters and the twist of the interest rate curve resulted in the following outcome:

**Table 11** Results of third simulation for 2010-2012_Optimisation and twist of interest rate

| 2010-2012: 1.Scenario, Twist_change of CDS spreads to originale state | | | | | |
|---|---|---|---|---|---|
| Increase of bond yields by | 2% | 5% | 7% | 10% | 20% |
| Twist of interest rate by | 2.00% | 5.00% | 7.00% | 10.00% | 20.00% |
| Belgium | -156.18% | -157.88% | -158.79% | -160.48% | -166.11% |
| Finland | -94.28% | -94.45% | -94.57% | -94.74% | -95.28% |
| France | 828.45% | 844.96% | 838.43% | 854.63% | 908.62% |
| Ireland | -224.98% | -222.99% | -221.14% | -219.16% | -212.53% |
| Italy | -140.72% | -141.32% | -141.67% | -142.28% | -144.30% |
| Netherlands | -837.15% | -836.95% | -834.50% | -834.31% | -833.66% |
| Portugal | -113.67% | -115.46% | -116.51% | -118.29% | -124.21% |
| Spain | -199.37% | -199.04% | -198.78% | -198.45% | -197.37% |
| Sweden | -83.07% | -89.52% | -93.84% | -100.29% | -121.77% |
| United Kingdom | 67.58% | 65.51% | 63.08% | 61.03% | 54.16% |

| 2010-2012: 2.Scenario, Twist_change of CDS spreads to originale state | | | | | |
|---|---|---|---|---|---|
| Increase of bond yields by | 2% | 5% | 7% | 10% | 20% |
| Twist of interest rate by | 2.00% | 5.00% | 7.00% | 10.00% | 20.00% |
| Belgium | -157.04% | -157.73% | -157.98% | -158.85% | -166.11% |
| Finland | -94.28% | -94.45% | -94.57% | -94.74% | -95.28% |
| France | 828.45% | 844.96% | 838.43% | 854.63% | 908.62% |
| Ireland | -224.98% | -222.99% | -221.14% | -219.16% | -217.63% |
| Italy | -140.72% | -141.32% | -141.67% | -142.28% | -144.30% |
| Netherlands | -837.15% | -836.95% | -834.50% | -834.31% | -833.66% |
| Portugal | -412.01% | -412.64% | -410.43% | -411.05% | -413.11% |
| Spain | -199.37% | -199.04% | -198.78% | -198.45% | -197.37% |
| Sweden | 167.35% | 166.00% | 164.59% | 163.24% | 158.76% |
| United Kingdom | 122.01% | 121.39% | 119.56% | 118.95% | 116.89% |

| 2010-2012: 3.Scenario, Twist_change of CDS spreads to originale state | | | | | |
|---|---|---|---|---|---|
| Increase of bond yields by | 2% | 5% | 7% | 10% | 20% |
| Twist of interest rate by | 2.00% | 5.00% | 7.00% | 10.00% | 20.00% |
| Belgium | -164.56% | -166.12% | -166.92% | -168.48% | -173.66% |
| Finland | -90.68% | -90.96% | -91.17% | -91.44% | -92.35% |
| France | 1154.79% | 1166.09% | 1150.26% | 1161.35% | 1198.30% |
| Ireland | -251.91% | -250.73% | -249.32% | -248.15% | -244.24% |
| Italy | -149.27% | -149.76% | -150.03% | -150.53% | -152.18% |
| Netherlands | -864.75% | -864.85% | -862.51% | -862.61% | -862.94% |
| Portugal | -409.63% | -410.26% | -408.07% | -408.69% | -410.75% |
| Spain | -242.95% | -241.83% | -241.02% | -239.90% | -236.17% |
| Sweden | 148.54% | 147.19% | 145.82% | 144.47% | 139.98% |
| United Kingdom | 120.81% | 120.17% | 118.34% | 117.70% | 115.58% |

| 2010-2012: 4.Scenario, Twist_change of CDS spreads to originale state | | | | | |
|---|---|---|---|---|---|
| Increase of bond yields by | 2% | 5% | 7% | 10% | 20% |
| Twist of interest rate by | 2.00% | 5.00% | 7.00% | 10.00% | 20.00% |
| Belgium | -164.56% | -166.12% | -166.92% | -168.48% | -173.66% |
| Finland | -90.68% | -90.96% | -91.17% | -91.44% | -92.35% |
| France | 1154.79% | 1166.09% | 1150.26% | 1161.35% | 1198.30% |
| Ireland | -251.91% | -250.73% | -249.32% | -248.15% | -244.24% |
| Italy | -149.27% | -149.76% | -150.03% | -150.53% | -152.18% |
| Netherlands | -864.75% | -864.85% | -862.51% | -862.61% | -862.94% |
| Portugal | -116.18% | -118.13% | -119.27% | -121.21% | -127.66% |
| Spain | -201.59% | -201.31% | -201.08% | -200.80% | -199.88% |
| Sweden | -31.77% | -29.90% | -28.80% | -26.94% | -20.73% |
| United Kingdom | 67.58% | 65.51% | 63.08% | 61.03% | 54.16% |

Incorporating the optimised parameters and the twist of the interest rate curves the same result as within the previous analysis regarding correlation including exceptions is given. The same is true for modest and high adaptations of CDS spread levels.

However, a different result as given for the first simulation is obtained for Finland, Portugal and Spain regarding the development of the CDS spread along with the increase of bond yields. Finland reverses changes for all scenarios so that CDS spreads increase within the third simulation. Portugal observes a change from decreasing to rising CDS spread modifications for the second and fourth scenario. Spain experiences reversed CDS spread changes within the first, second and third scenario. In case of Finland, the development of the CDS spreads corresponds to the development given for a twist shift of interest rates.

Comparing the levels of CDS spread changes to the first simulation, the CDS spread changes decrease for Netherlands within all scenarios. In addition, Spain observes declining spreads within the first and second scenario. In the third scenario, Sweden and United Kingdom experience a decrease, whereas in the fourth scenario lower CDS spread changes are given for Portugal and Spain. However, mainly the CDS spread changes increase within all scenarios. Comparing the levels of CDS spread changes to the second simulation, a decrease of changes is given for Belgium, Ireland, Italy and Portugal. Higher changes of spreads are observed for Finland, France, Netherlands, Spain, Sweden and United Kingdom.

Thus, comparing the first or respectively the second simulation with the given one an increase of CDS spread changes is commonly observed.

For the second sample period following results incorporating the optimisation of parameters and the parallel shift of the interest rate curve are obtained:

**Table 12** Results of third simulation for 2013-2015_Parallel shift of interest rate

| 2013-2015: 1.Scenario, Shift_change of CDS spreads to originale state | | | | | |
|---|---|---|---|---|---|
| Increase of bond yields by | 2% | 5% | 7% | 10% | 20% |
| Parallel shift of interest rate | 0.20% | 0.50% | 0.70% | 1.00% | 2.00% |
| Belgium | -103.20% | -102.79% | -102.52% | -102.10% | -100.74% |
| Finland | -95.52% | -95.97% | -95.23% | -95.79% | -97.67% |
| France | 223.11% | 220.28% | 206.71% | 203.98% | 194.89% |
| Ireland | -108.03% | -107.84% | -107.77% | -107.58% | -106.94% |
| Italy | -254.81% | -253.54% | -252.33% | -251.07% | -246.87% |
| Netherlands | -120.47% | -120.44% | -120.31% | -120.28% | -120.18% |
| Portugal | -92.33% | -90.86% | -89.81% | -88.34% | -83.41% |
| Spain | -104.55% | -104.22% | -103.64% | -103.34% | -102.33% |
| Sweden | -100.50% | -100.78% | -100.96% | -101.24% | -102.18% |
| United Kingdom | -114.06% | -114.31% | -114.36% | -114.61% | -115.44% |

| 2013-2015: 2.Scenario, Shift_change of CDS spreads to originale state | | | | | |
|---|---|---|---|---|---|
| Increase of bond yields by | 2% | 5% | 7% | 10% | 20% |
| Parallel shift of interest rate | 0.20% | 0.50% | 0.70% | 1.00% | 2.00% |
| Belgium | -104.86% | -104.47% | -104.22% | -103.84% | -102.57% |
| Finland | -37.54% | -37.39% | -19.96% | -19.77% | -19.13% |
| France | 336.36% | 337.01% | 321.41% | 322.03% | 324.13% |
| Ireland | -162.18% | -162.35% | -162.93% | -163.10% | -163.67% |
| Italy | -254.81% | -253.54% | -252.33% | -251.07% | -246.87% |
| Netherlands | -82.97% | -82.99% | -83.10% | -83.12% | -83.19% |
| Portugal | -69.69% | -69.58% | -69.33% | -69.22% | -68.88% |
| Spain | -150.28% | -150.13% | -145.63% | -145.50% | -145.05% |
| Sweden | -74.21% | -74.03% | -74.07% | -73.89% | -73.29% |
| United Kingdom | -71.31% | -71.39% | -71.67% | -71.75% | -72.03% |

| 2013-2015: 3.Scenario, Shift_change of CDS spreads to originale state | | | | | |
|---|---|---|---|---|---|
| Increase of bond yields by | 2% | 5% | 7% | 10% | 20% |
| Parallel shift of interest rate | 0.20% | 0.50% | 0.70% | 1.00% | 2.00% |
| Belgium | -102.22% | -101.80% | -101.53% | -101.11% | -99.73% |
| Finland | -85.31% | -85.06% | -80.71% | -80.39% | -79.32% |
| France | 224.27% | 221.45% | 207.84% | 205.12% | 196.04% |
| Ireland | -108.06% | -107.87% | -107.80% | -107.61% | -106.97% |
| Italy | -255.57% | -254.32% | -253.11% | -251.87% | -247.71% |
| Netherlands | -120.47% | -120.44% | -120.31% | -120.28% | -120.18% |
| Portugal | -91.27% | -89.83% | -88.77% | -87.27% | -82.27% |
| Spain | -104.62% | -104.29% | -103.71% | -103.40% | -102.40% |
| Sweden | -99.88% | -100.16% | -100.34% | -100.62% | -101.53% |
| United Kingdom | -115.27% | -115.52% | -115.57% | -115.82% | -116.65% |

| 2013-2015: 4.Scenario, Shift_change of CDS spreads to originale state | | | | | |
|---|---|---|---|---|---|
| Increase of bond yields by | 2% | 5% | 7% | 10% | 20% |
| Parallel shift of interest rate | 0.20% | 0.50% | 0.70% | 1.00% | 2.00% |
| Belgium | -93.12% | -92.86% | -92.69% | -92.44% | -91.59% |
| Finland | -44.10% | -43.95% | -28.33% | -28.14% | -27.50% |
| France | 348.74% | 349.27% | 333.14% | 333.65% | 335.36% |
| Ireland | -175.57% | -175.74% | -176.42% | -176.59% | -177.16% |
| Italy | -215.56% | -215.57% | -215.29% | -215.30% | -215.32% |
| Netherlands | -96.41% | -96.43% | -96.46% | -96.48% | -96.55% |
| Portugal | -96.68% | -96.57% | -96.48% | -96.38% | -96.03% |
| Spain | -154.99% | -154.84% | -149.92% | -149.79% | -149.34% |
| Sweden | -78.97% | -79.02% | -79.18% | -79.23% | -79.39% |
| United Kingdom | -80.73% | -80.82% | -81.02% | -81.10% | -81.38% |

Within the second sample period, incorporating the optimised parameters and the parallel shift of the interest rate curve a negative correlation between bond yields and CDS spreads excluding France is given.

Modest CDS spread changes are given for Finland and Portugal for all scenarios. Netherlands, Sweden and United Kingdom examine a moderate change of CDS spreads in the second, fourth and respectively in the third scenario in case of Sweden. Significant adaption of CDS spreads is observed for France and Italy within all scenarios.

Investigating the development of the CDS spread along with the increase of bond yields and parallel shift of interest rate a quite similar result compared to the first simulation is given. Solely the CDS spread change of

Italy and Sweden within the second scenario is reversed compared to the first simulation.

Comparing the levels of CDS spread changes to the first simulation, the CDS spread changes decreases for Ireland, Italy, Netherlands, Sweden and United Kingdom within all scenarios. An increase of CDS spread changes is observed for Belgium, Finland, France, Portugal and Spain. Hence, a balance of countries which increase or respectively decrease their CDS spreads is given. Comparing the levels of CDS spread changes to the second simulation, a decrease of changes is given for Belgium, Ireland, Italy, Portugal and Spain for all scenarios. In addition, Netherlands observes declining CDS spreads within the second scenario. As only Finland, France, Sweden, United Kingdom and Netherlands experience increasing CDS spreads excluding the second scenario the majority of the countries decrease their CDS spread changes.

Incorporating the optimisation of parameters and the twist of the interest rate curve following outcome is received:

**Table 13** Results of third simulation for 2013-2015_Twist of interest rate

| 2013-2015: 1.Scenario, Twist_change of CDS spreads to originale state | | | | | |
|---|---|---|---|---|---|
| Increase of bond yields by | 2% | 5% | 7% | 10% | 20% |
| Twist of interest rate by | 2.00% | 5.00% | 7.00% | 10.00% | 20.00% |
| Belgium | -103.14% | -102.63% | -102.30% | -101.79% | -100.11% |
| Finland | -95.49% | -95.87% | -95.06% | -95.56% | -97.20% |
| France | 223.24% | 220.60% | 207.15% | 204.61% | 196.14% |
| Ireland | -108.08% | -107.95% | -107.92% | -107.79% | -107.36% |
| Italy | -254.81% | -253.55% | -252.34% | -251.08% | -246.88% |
| Netherlands | -120.48% | -120.45% | -120.33% | -120.31% | -120.23% |
| Portugal | -92.30% | -90.79% | -89.73% | -88.21% | -83.16% |
| Spain | -104.52% | -104.13% | -103.53% | -103.18% | -102.00% |
| Sweden | -100.51% | -100.81% | -101.01% | -101.30% | -102.29% |
| United Kingdom | -114.08% | -114.36% | -114.43% | -114.71% | -115.64% |

| 2013-2015: 2.Scenario, Twist_change of CDS spreads to originale state | | | | | |
|---|---|---|---|---|---|
| Increase of bond yields by | 2% | 5% | 7% | 10% | 20% |
| Twist of interest rate by | 2.00% | 5.00% | 7.00% | 10.00% | 20.00% |
| Belgium | -104.79% | -104.32% | -104.00% | -103.53% | -101.94% |
| Finland | -37.51% | -37.30% | -19.80% | -19.53% | -18.66% |
| France | 336.49% | 337.34% | 321.84% | 322.66% | 325.38% |
| Ireland | -162.22% | -162.45% | -163.08% | -163.31% | -164.08% |
| Italy | -254.81% | -253.55% | -252.34% | -251.08% | -246.88% |
| Netherlands | -82.98% | -83.01% | -83.11% | -83.14% | -83.24% |
| Portugal | -69.66% | -69.52% | -69.24% | -69.10% | -68.63% |
| Spain | -150.24% | -150.04% | -145.51% | -145.33% | -144.72% |
| Sweden | -74.23% | -74.06% | -74.11% | -73.95% | -73.41% |
| United Kingdom | -71.33% | -71.44% | -71.74% | -71.85% | -72.23% |

| 2013-2015: 3.Scenario, Twist_change of CDS spreads to originale state | | | | | |
|---|---|---|---|---|---|
| Increase of bond yields by | 2% | 5% | 7% | 10% | 20% |
| Twist of interest rate by | 2.00% | 5.00% | 7.00% | 10.00% | 20.00% |
| Belgium | -102.16% | -101.65% | -101.31% | -100.80% | -99.10% |
| Finland | -85.27% | -84.97% | -80.55% | -80.16% | -78.84% |
| France | 224.40% | 221.77% | 208.28% | 205.75% | 197.30% |
| Ireland | -108.10% | -107.97% | -107.94% | -107.82% | -107.38% |
| Italy | -255.57% | -254.32% | -253.12% | -251.87% | -247.72% |
| Netherlands | -120.48% | -120.45% | -120.33% | -120.31% | -120.23% |
| Portugal | -91.25% | -89.77% | -88.68% | -87.14% | -82.02% |
| Spain | -104.58% | -104.19% | -103.59% | -103.24% | -102.07% |
| Sweden | -99.89% | -100.19% | -100.38% | -100.68% | -101.65% |
| United Kingdom | -115.29% | -115.57% | -115.64% | -115.92% | -116.85% |

| 2013-2015: 4.Scenario, Twist_change of CDS spreads to originale state | | | | | |
|---|---|---|---|---|---|
| Increase of bond yields by | 2% | 5% | 7% | 10% | 20% |
| Twist of interest rate by | 2.00% | 5.00% | 7.00% | 10.00% | 20.00% |
| Belgium | -93.05% | -92.70% | -92.47% | -92.12% | -90.96% |
| Finland | -44.06% | -43.86% | -28.17% | -27.90% | -27.03% |
| France | 348.87% | 349.60% | 333.58% | 334.28% | 336.61% |
| Ireland | -175.61% | -175.84% | -176.57% | -176.80% | -177.58% |
| Italy | -215.56% | -215.57% | -215.30% | -215.31% | -215.33% |
| Netherlands | -96.41% | -96.44% | -96.48% | -96.51% | -96.60% |
| Portugal | -96.65% | -96.51% | -96.39% | -96.25% | -95.78% |
| Spain | -154.95% | -154.75% | -149.81% | -149.63% | -149.01% |
| Sweden | -78.98% | -79.05% | -79.22% | -79.29% | -79.51% |
| United Kingdom | -80.75% | -80.87% | -81.09% | -81.20% | -81.58% |

Combining optimised parameters and the twist of the interest rate curves a negative correlation between bond yields and CDS spreads is still prevailing. Similar results as within the previous analysis are obtained for modest and high changes of CDS spread levels.

The development of the CDS spread along with the increase of bond yields and twist of interest rate only causes changes for two countries compared to the first simulation. As the case by combining optimised parameters and the parallel shift of the interest rate curves, only Italy and Sweden observe a reversion of CDS spread changes within the second scenario.

Comparing the levels of CDS spread changes to the first simulation, the CDS spread changes decrease for Ireland, Italy, Netherlands, Sweden and United Kingdom within all scenarios. An increase of CDS spread changes is observed for Belgium, Finland, France, Portugal and Spain. Thus, the same changes compared to the first simulation are given combining optimised parameters with a parallel or respectively a twist of the interest rate curve. The same is true for the comparison of the second and the third simulation. Hence, comparing the CDS spread changes to the second simulation a decline of CDS spread changes for the majority of countries is observed.

# 5 Results

After having conducted the simulations, the results for each country regarding the initial stated research questions can be discussed.

Given the model of Belgium, a spread increase of government bonds negatively impacts CDS spreads for both periods. A change of bond yields triggers a substantial movement of CDS spreads. Hence, the different increase levels results in changes of CDS spreads of around -160.13% to -165.32% on average for the first period. Within the second sample period, CDS spread changes around -101.02% to -100.35%. Thus, within the first sample period CDS spread changes increase with higher bond yields, whereas in the second period a diverging development is given.

Further, the simulations exhibits that the risk-free rate factor does not substantially influence CDS spread changes more than other risk factors within the models. However, in the first sample period an increase of CDS spread changes incorporating risk-free rate in the optimisation is observed. Given the second period, a decrease of changes for the first two scenarios and an increase for the last two scenarios are observed including the risk-free rate. Yet, on average a decrease of CDS spread changes is observed for the second sample period.

Investigating the impact of increasing bond yields further, it is examined that the impact of increasing bond yields flattens within the first sample period for the increase levels of 10% and 20%. However, a decreasing impact is not observed for the given increase levels. By contrast, a declining impact of increasing bond yields is observed for the second sample period.

Comparing the two sample periods, it is observed that the first sample period experience significantly higher CDS spread changes than the second period. Hence, higher CDS spreads are given for the lower interest rate environment in the second sample period.

A negative relationship between rising government bond yields and credit default swap spreads is given for Finland for both periods. Within the first period minor CDS spread changes of around -92.29% to -91.92% are experienced. A lower level of CDS spread changes of approximately -65.72% to -57.18% is observed from 2013 to 2015. Hence, increasing bond yields result in decreasing CDS spread changes.

Incorporating the risk-free rate factor in the optimisation higher CDS spread changes are given in the first two scenarios, whereas lower changes are observed in the third and fourth scenario for the first sample period. Within the second period increasing CDS spread changes are given excluding the first scenario. On average, incorporating the risk-free rate results in an increase of CDS spread changes for the first period, whereas a decrease is experienced in the second sample period.

Further, it is observed that within the first sample period the impact of increased bond yields substantially declines between an increase level of 7% to 10% and continues to remain on the same level for higher bond yield increases. Within the second sample period, a major decrease of CDS spread changes is given between an increase level of 5% to 7%. Subsequently, an increase of changes is observed. Thus, a diminishing impact of bond yield increases is observed for the first period, whereas in the second period a declining impact followed by an inferior increase is given.

Comparing the results of CDS spread changes for both sample periods, it is observed that the first sample period experiences higher CDS spread changes than the second period.

In case of France, a positive relationship between increasing bond yields and CDS spread changes is given. Major CDS spread changes of 991.75% to 1054.66% on average are observed for the first period. Within the second sample period significantly lower CDS spread changes of 282.77% to 259.19% on average are given. Thus, overall CDS spread changes move along with bond yield increases from 2010 to 2015, whereas a diverging movement is observed for the second sample period.

Including risk-free rate within the optimisation process, higher CDS spread changes are observed for the first period. Declining CDS spread changes are given for 2013 to 2015.

Investigating the impact of increasing bond yields further, it is observed that a substantial decrease of CDS spread changes is given between an increase level of 5% to 7% for bond yields in the first sample period. However, bond yields higher than 7% experience a reverse impact of a similar high level. Thus, the decrease is equalised by higher increase levels. Within the second sample period, an even higher decrease of CDS spread changes is observed between an increase level of 5% to 7%. Declining CDS spread changes are still given for higher increase levels, yet on a substantially smaller basis.

A tremendous difference between levels of CDS spread changes is given between the first and second sample period for France. Thus, the second period observes CDS spread changes of a fourth of the changes experienced in the first period.

Given the model of Ireland, a spread increase of government bonds negatively affects CDS spreads for both periods. Changes of around -238.10% to -226.18% on average are observed in the first period, whereas CDS spread changes of approximately -138.35% to -137.55% are given in the second sample period. Thus, increasing bond yields result in decreasing CDS spread changes for both periods.

Incorporating the risk-free rate, an increase of CDS spread changes for the first sample period is given. By contrast, the second period experiences a decline of changes.

A steady decrease of CDS spread changes by increasing bond yields is given for the first sample period. Within the second sample period a minor increase of CDS spread changes on average is given between a bond increase of 5% to 7%. Higher bond yield increase levels experience a slight decrease of CDS spread changes.

Comparing the results of CDS spread changes for both sample periods, higher CDS spread changes are observed in the first sample period. The second period experiences CDS spread changes of nearly the half of the changes given in the first period.

A negative relationship between rising government bond yields and credit default swap spreads is observed for Italy in both periods. Given the first sample period, CDS spread changes around -144.92% to -147.54% are examined. Higher changes around -245.18% to -239.15% are given for the second period. Thus, CDS spread changes move along with bond yield increases in the first sample period, whereas a diverging movement is observed from 2013 to 2015.

Involving all risk factors in the optimisation, increasing CDS spread changes are given for both sample periods.

Investigating the impact of increasing bond yields further, an augmenting increase along with increasing bond yields can be observed for the first sample period. By contrast, a decrease of CDS spread changes along with higher bond yields is observed from 2013 to 2015. Given higher increase levels for bond yields, a convergence of the declining basis to a stable level is examined.

Comparing both sample periods, higher CDS spread change levels are observed within the second sample period. Thus, a lower interest rate environment results in higher CDS spread changes for Italy.

In case of Netherlands, a negative relatedness between increasing bond yields and CDS spread changes is given. Decreasing CDS spread changes of approximately -851.09% to -849.69% are experienced in the first sample period. By contrast, smaller changes around -105.07% to -104.97% are observed for the second period. A diverging development of CDS spread changes to increasing bond yields is given for both periods.

Modest higher CDS spread changes are observed incorporating the risk-free rate in the optimisation for both periods. Yet, the impact of involving all factors is significantly higher for the first period.

Analysing the impact of increasing bond yields in more detail, it can be observed that a substantial decrease of CDS spread changes is given between an increase level of 5% to 7% for bond yields in the first sample period. Higher bond yields result in minor increasing CDS spread changes. Within the second sample period, a declining decrease of CDS spread changes along with higher bond yields is experienced.

A substantial decrease of the level of CDS spread change is observed between the first and second sample period. Thus, for a lower interest rate environment significantly lower CDS spread changes in case of Netherlands are given.

Given the model of Portugal, a spread increase of government bonds negatively impacts CDS spreads in both periods. CDS spread changes around -262.46% to -264.81% are examined within the first sample period. Lower changes around -87.56% to -83.34% are given for the second period. Thus, CDS spread changes move along with bond yield increases in the first sample period, whereas a diverging movement is observed from 2013 to 2015.

Involving all risk factors in the optimisation process higher CDS spread changes are given in the first sample period, whereas slightly lower CDS spread changes are experienced in the second period.

From 2010 to 2012 a decrease of CDS spread changes is given between an increase level of 5% to 7% for bond yields followed by an increase at a stable level. A declining decrease of CDS spread changes is given within the second sample period.

Comparing the results of CDS spread changes for both sample periods, significantly higher CDS spread changes for the first sample period are observed.

A negative relationship between rising government bond yields and credit default swap spreads is observed for Spain for both periods. Given the different increase level changes of CDS spreads of around -211.56% to -215.16% on average for the first period are observed. Within the second sample period, CDS spread changes around -128.71% to -125.67%. Thus, within the first sample period CDS spread changes increase with higher bond yields, whereas in the second period a diverging development is given.

Incorporating the risk-free rate in the optimisation an inferior increase of CDS spread changes is observed.

Investigating the impact of increasing bond yields further, a steady increase of CDS spread changes along with increasing bond yields can be observed for the first sample period. However, higher bond yields lead to a flattening of the impact. Within the second sample period a substantial decrease of CDS spread changes on average is given between a bond increase of 5% to 7%. Higher bond yields cause minor decreasing CDS spread changes.

Comparing the results of CDS spread changes for both sample periods, higher CDS spread changes are observed from 2010 to 2012. The second period experiences CDS spread changes of nearly the half of the changes given in the first period.

In case of Sweden a negative relatedness between increasing bond yields and CDS spread changes for the first period is given in the first and third scenario, whereas a positive relation is observed in the second and fourth scenario. By contrast, within the second sample period a spread increase of government bond negatively affects CDS spreads in all scenarios.

Given a negative correlation increasing CDS spread changes of approximately -56.52% to -62.28% are experienced in the first sample period. By contrast, changes around 158.85% to 158.34% are observed for positive relatedness. Within the second sample period CDS spread changes around -88.36% to -88.77% on average are given. Hence, an increase of changes in case of positive correlation are experienced, whereas in case of negative correlation a slight decrease of changes is examined.

Modest lower CDS spread changes are observed incorporating the risk-free rate in the optimisation if a negative relationship of bond yields to CDS spread changes is prevailing. By contrast, a slight increase of CDS spread changes is given for positive relatedness.

Analysing the impact of increasing bond yields in more detail, a steady increase of CDS spread changes which declines with higher bond yields is observed for the first sample period if negative correlation is given. In case of positive relatedness, a decrease is experienced between an increase level for bond yields of 5% to 7%. Higher bond yields do not influence CDS spread changes further due to the minimisation. Within the second period a steady increase of CDS spread changes which flattens with increasing bond yields is observed.

Given the different correlation within the first sample period a comparison to the second sample period is not possible.

Given the model of United Kingdom, a spread increase of government bonds positively impacts CDS spreads within the first sample period, whereas a negative correlation is observed in the second sample period. Changes of around 94.93% to 89.45% on average are observed in the first period, whereas CDS spread changes of approximately -95.29% to -95.83% are given in the second sample period. Thus, increasing bond yields result in decreasing CDS spread changes for 2010 to 2012. Within the second sample period a slight increase of CDS spread changes along with higher bond yields is given.

Incorporating the risk-free rate a slight increase of CDS spread changes in both periods is experienced.

From 2010 to 2012 a steady decrease of CDS spread changes is given. However, higher bond yields cause a decline of the decreasing impact. Within the second sample period the increase level of CDS spread changes declines with higher bond yields. A flattening of the impact of increasing bond yields is recognised between the increase levels of 10% to 20% for bond yields.

Comparing the results of CDS spread changes similar spread changes are observed for both sample periods. However, the CDS spread changes are of opposite direction as the signs varies.

# 6 Concluding remarks

Within this thesis the relationship between government bond yields and credit default swaps has been investigated. Therefore, first the constituents of credit default swap spreads have been examined in detail by modelling CDS spreads according to Hull and White. The calculation evidenced that the risk-neutral probabilities of default which further depends on the chosen recovery rate highly influence the results. Moreover, results based on a shorter time frame experienced higher significance.

Examining the impact of increased government bond yields on credit default swaps based on the model of Fontana and Scheicher, it has been observed that the impact substantially varies between countries within the European area. Frequently a negative relatedness between government bond yields and credit default swap spreads is given. Exemptions thereof are France, Sweden and United Kingdom. Incorporating the risk-free rate factor in the optimisation commonly higher CDS spread changes are observed in the first sample period, whereas lower changes are given in the second period. Within the first period, CDS spread changes move along with increasing bond yields excluding Ireland, Netherlands, Sweden and United Kingdom. In case of Sweden and United Kingdom lower CDS spread changes for higher bond yields are observed for a positive correlation. Within the second period, a diverging movement of CDS spread changes to bond yields is given. Exemptions thereof are Sweden and United Kingdom.

Further analysis examined whether the impact of an increase of bond yields flatten or even diminish. Within the first period an indifferent development is given for the various countries. By contrast, within the second sample period frequently a decrease is observed. A flattening of the decrease starting around an increase level for bond yields of 7% is recognised.

In order to investigate whether the prevailing interest rate environment has a substantial effect on the impact of increasing bond yields, a comparison of both sample periods has been conducted. Thus, it is observed that frequently lower CDS spread changes move along with the lower interest rate environment. Solely in the case of Italy higher CDS spread changes are observed. A comparison of the two sample periods for Sweden and United Kingdom is not possible due to the change of correlation.

Hence it is observed that within a lower interest rate environment CDS spreads correspondingly change on a lower scale. However, a stable change of signs for CDS spreads given negative interest rates is not observed.

Moreover, given the model of Fontana and Scheicher, it is clearly experienced that the risk-free rate factor only accounts for a small portion. Thus, an adaption of the CDS spreads is faster experienced for other risk factors. However, a long-term change of interest rates influence the CDS spreads substantially as observed within the second simulation.

Thus, further analysis investigating specifically the development of CDS spreads within low interest rates should be conducted in order to give an outlook for a low interest rate environment.

The results of this thesis, however, have to be treated carefully as the used models are based on several assumptions. Thus, further research applying the model of Fontana and Scheicher using advanced regression methods can be done. Furthermore, within the analysis government bonds of Germany are used as benchmark. Alternatively, spot rates can be used as certain studies argue that spot rates are a better proxy for the benchmark.[53] Moreover, within the thesis the impact of varying government bond yields on CDS spreads is investigated. Prevailing literature verifies that this direction of relationship is given for Europe and Asia[54], however, given other countries it has been experienced that commonly the CDS markets tend to guide fixed income markets regarding price movements.[55] Indeed, studies already argue that since the financial crisis the credit derivative market leads the bond market which has been also observed for sovereign markets. [56] This also explains the high CDS spread changes observed within the simulations. Hence, further research

53 Houweling/ Vorst (2005), pp. 1200-1223.
54 Zhu (2006), pp. 228-234.
55 Rubia et al. (2015), p.228.
56 Delatte et al. (2012), p. 488.

whether the CDS markets guide the bond market in Europe after the financial crisis and the sovereign debt crisis can be conducted.

# References

Alexopoulou, I./ Andersson, M./ Georgescu, O. (2009): An empirical study on the decoupling movements between corporate bond and CDS spreads, European Central Bank: Working Paper Series, 1085, pp. 1-36, retrieved from: https://www.ecb.europa.eu/pub/pdf/scpwps/ecbwp1085.pdf?09e4c58bd689f2d08f8c28e1ad0496a6, accessed 18.04.20016

Amato, J./ Remolona, E. (2003): The credit spread puzzle, in: BIS Quarterly Review, pp. 51-63

Ammer, J./ Cai, F. (2007): Sovereign CDS and Bond Pricing Dynamics in Emerging Markets: Does Cheapest-to-Deliver Option Matter?, Board of Governors of the Federal Reserve System, 912, pp. 1-44, retrieved from: https://www.federalreserve.gov/pubs/ifdp/2007/912/ifdp912.pdf, accessed 17.04.2016

Blanco, R./ Brennan, S./ Marsh,I. (2005): An Empirical analysis of the dynamic relation between Investment-Grade Bonds and Credit Default Swaps, in: The Journal of Finance, 60/5, pp. 2255-2281

Calice, G./ Chenb, J./ Williams, J. (2013): Liquidity spillovers in sovereign bond and CDS markets: An analysis of the Eurozone sovereign debt crisis, in: Journal of Economic Behavior and Organization, 85, pp. 122–143

Carol, A. (2008): Market Risk Analysis, Volume 1, 1st ed., England: John Wiley and Sons

Codogno, L./ Favero, C./ Missale, A. (2003): Yield spreads on EMU government bonds, in: Economic Policy, 18/37, pp. 503-532, retrieved from: http://www.jstor.org/stable/1344743?seq=1#page_scan_tab_contents, accessed 18.04.2016

Delatte, A./ Gex, M./ López-Villavicencio, A.(2012): Has the CDS market influenced the borrowing cost of European countries during the sovereign crisis?, in: Journal of International Money and Finance, 31/3, pp. 481-497

Duffie, D. (1998): Credit Swap Valuation, working paper, pp. 1-30, retrieved from: http://www.worldscientific.com/doi/abs/10.1142/S0219024906003445; accessed 17.04.2016

Duffie, D. (1999): Credit Swap Valuation, in: Financial Analysts Journal, pp. 73-87

Fontana, A./ Scheicher, M. (2010): An Analysis of Euro Area sovereign CDS and their relation with government bonds, European Central Bank: Working Paper Series, 1271, pp. 1-49, retrieved from: https://www.ecb.europa.eu/pub/pdf/scpwps/ecbwp1271.pdf?679eaae7fe76ff71f896b1b7c26b8032, accessed 17.04.2016

Gapen, M./ Gray, D./ Lim, C./ Xiao, Y. (2008): Measuring and analyzing sovereign risk with contingent claims, IMF Staff Papers, 55/1, pp. 109-148, retrieved from: http://www.jstor.org/stable/30035939?seq=1# page_scan_tab_contents, accesed 18.04.2016

Gündüz, Y./ Kayab, O. (2014): Impacts of the financial crisis on Eurozone sovereign CDS spreads, in: Journal of International Money and Finance, 49/B, pp. 425-442

Houweling, P./ Vorst, T. (2005): Pricing default swaps: Empirical evidence, in: Journal of International Money and Finance, 24, pp 1200-1225

Hull, J (2012): Options, future and other derivatives, 8th ed., England: Pearson

Hull, J./ Predescu, M./ White, A. (2004): The relationship between credit default swap spreads, bond yields, and credit rating announcements, in: Journal of Banking and Finance, 28/11, pp. 2789–2811

Hull, J./ White, A.(2000): Valuing Credit Default Swaps I: No Counterparty Default Risk, in: Journal of Derivatives, 8/1, pp. 29-40

Longstaff, F./ Mithal, S./ Neis, E. (2003): The credit-default swap market: Is credit protection priced correctly?,Working paper,pp. 1-47,retrieved from:http://www.usc.edu/schools/business/FBE/seminars/papers/F_10-24-03_LONGSTAFF_cdsnew.pdf,accessed 18.04.2016

Merton, R. (1974): On the pricing of corporate debt: the risk structure of interest rates, The Journal of Finance, 29/2, pp. 449-470

Meissner, G. (2005): Credit Derivatives: Application, Pricing and Risk Management , 1st ed., United Kingdom: Blackwell Publishing

Palladini, G./ Portes, R. (2011): Sovereign CDS and Bond pricing dynamics in the Euro-Area, NBER Working Paper Series,17586, pp. 1-35, retrieved from: http://www.nber.org/papers/w17586.pdf, accessed 18.04.2016

Rubia, A./ Sanchis-Marco L./ Serrano P. (2015): Market frictions and the pricing of sovereign credit default swaps, in Journal of International Money and Finance, 60, pp. 223-252

Schönbuchner, P. (2003): Credit derivatives pricing models: models, pricing and implementation ,1st ed., England: John Wiley and Sons

Zhu, H. (2006): An Empirical Comparison of Credit Spreads between the Bond Market and the Credit Default Swap Market, in: Journal of Financial Services Research, 29/3, pp. 211-235